D0268973

CAVENDISH PRACTICE NOTES

ONE WEEK LOAN

AND

Cavendish
Publishing
Limited

London • Sydney

Fourth edition first published in Great Britain 2001 by Cavendish Publishing Limited, The Glass House, Wharton Street, London WC1X 9PX, United Kingdom

Telephone: +44 (0)20 7278 8000   Facsimile: +44 (0)20 7278 8080

Email: info@cavendishpublishing.com

Website: www.cavendishpublishing.com

© Coates, R and Attwell, N   2001

British Library Cataloguing in Publication Data

Coates, Ross
Conveyancing – 4th ed – (Practice notes series)
1 Conveyancing – England 2 Conveyancing – Wales
I Title II Attwell, Nicholas
346.4'2'0438

ISBN 1 85941 453 2

Printed and bound in Great Britain

Contents

1 Introduction

This book is intended to guide the practitioner through the labyrinth of conveyancing practice, and to enable the reader to carry out most types of property transaction, whether they be freehold or leasehold, or whether they be commercial or residential.

The increasing demands of the public for the conveyancing transaction to be faster and to be kept informed at every stage, combined with the increasing pace at which technology evolves, means that the art and practice of conveyancing is forever changing. It is probably true to say that at no previous time has there been such a challenging business environment for the conveyancer to face.

1.1 Establishing a conveyancing practice

The establishment of a conveyancing practice, whether as a licensed conveyancer or as a solicitor, not only depends on successful networking in order to obtain work from a variety of contacts, but increasingly depends on successful marketing followed up with a high quality service.

Quite apart from one's technical ability, the following steps, which are carefully laid out in this book, set out some basic practical common sense skills which are required in order to build and to sustain a successful conveyancing practice.

It is important to move transactions forward quickly, because most clients will place great emphasis on speed. For them, that will be the quality of the service. It is equally important to be responsive to telephone calls and to correspondence as quickly as possible. The majority of complaints by the public against conveyancers emanate from basic day to day practices such as the failure to return telephone calls, rather than any technical deficiency on the part of the conveyancer. The successful handling of telephone calls and emails and computer literacy represent the hallmark of a successful and thriving modern conveyancing practice.

In recent years, with fierce price competition and the developments in technology, conveyancing practitioners have sought to brand their practices in one of two ways: as a 'conveyancing factory'; or as a 'property shop'. The 'conveyancing factory' model is based on the premise that clients are willing to conduct their conveyancing transaction without coming face to face with their conveyancer. Setting up a 'conveyancing factory' involves great expenditure on technology, competitive fees, and fee-earners who have good computer and communication skills. The 'property shop' model aims to secure the incoming work for the conveyancer by entering the property selling business in order to create a relationship with the client from the outset of the client's property experience. The 'property shop' model also envisages the estate agent, surveyor, letting agent, mortgage adviser and conveyancer working closely together to offer their client a better service. This concept has been around for 10 years or more, but it is only recently that it appears to be coming to fruition.

However one chooses to set up a conveyancing practice, all successful firms have to address two important developments: technology and marketing.

1.1.1 Technology

Technology has played a vital part in the development of all legal practices. It is now becoming the norm for a computer to be found on every fee-earner's desktop. However, residential conveyancing in particular has been an area of practice which can be systemised to a much greater extent. Most firms now have standard house style documents and a case management system which dovetails with accounts software. Some of the larger firms have developed intranet knowledge systems. An intranet is a large firm-wide database which stores legal knowhow which the conveyancer can then use from his desktop without having to go to books or journals.

Technology has also played an important role in other aspects of the office. In finding new work, the Internet has offered a cheap opportunity to advertise globally. However, in order to develop and retain brand loyalty, Internet advertising must be coupled with other more traditional forms of marketing such as referrals, newspaper and radio. The Internet also provides the environment in which some firms have chosen to offer clients online progress reports.

Internal and external office communication has been revolutionised by the introduction of email. Email offers real time written communication from the desktop at cheaper rates than most telephone calls. It also provides a simple and fast way for a principal to communicate with his staff wherever in the world they may be. In larger firms, it is noticeable that email as a form of communication is beginning to replace the telephone and fax.

Developments in technology to watch in the future are voice activated word-processing products, electronic signatures and deal rooms. If voice activated word processing can be made to work competently, then it could spell the end of the traditional role of the secretary. The Electronic Communications Act 2000 recognised, for the first time, the concept of the 'electronic signature' which, in time, will replace the physical signature. This should assist in the process of electronic conveyancing. Deal rooms will offer parties to a property transaction the opportunity to meet online and negotiate and amend documentation.

1.1.2 Marketing

Conveyancing practices, like much of the legal profession, have been slow to promote and market themselves actively, relying instead upon the age old technique of 'reputation' and 'word of mouth'. In recent years, this has changed. Conveyancing firms are more actively promoting the services they offer in all manner of media, including the Internet, television, radio and newspaper. Many of the larger firms now actually have marketing departments comprising staff trained in this area of expertise.

Linked closely with marketing is the idea of branding. It has been noticeable in the last couple of years that many firms have sought to rebrand themselves so that they offer a fresh, modern image. When branding, it is important to protect your brand image through trade mark and domain name registration.

2 Basic Information

2.1 Introduction

Conveyancing is the process which is implemented in order to sell either a freehold or leasehold interest in land.

2.1.1 Registered and unregistered conveyancing

Depending upon whether the seller's interest in land is registered at the Land Registry, there are two systems of conveyancing: registered and unregistered.

Despite the fact that registered conveyancing was introduced in 1925, it was not until 1 December 1990 that the whole of England and Wales became compulsorily registrable. In 1998, it became necessary to apply for registration of land acquired by gift or will, and now over 80% of all titles are registered.

In essence, registered conveyancing has replaced the traditional bundle of title deeds with a certificate of ownership known either as a land certificate or a charge certificate, depending on whether or not there is a subsisting mortgage. The conveyancing transaction is only completed when the dealing is registered at the appropriate Land Registry on the payment of an appropriate fee.

For the purposes of this book, we have decided not to deal with the art of unregistered conveyancing.

2.2 Conveyancing practice

The National Conveyancing Protocol was introduced by the Law Society on 21 March 1990 under the logo 'TransAction'. These procedures apply to residential transactions only. The National Protocol requires the seller's solicitor to deposit a comprehensive package of documentation with the buyer's solicitor at the outset, and the original theory was that this would speed up the conveyancing process. In reality, the National Protocol has not greatly accelerated the conveyancing process, because so much of the speed also depends upon the availability of mortgage finance and the synchronisation of a prospective client's personal requirements in any given chain of transactions. The same concerns are also being levelled at the latest initiative to speed up conveyancing – the seller's pack.

One of the significant factors of employing a solicitor or licensed conveyancer to deal with conveyancing transactions is the fact that they can use undertakings at certain pivotal stages of the transaction in order to enable the transaction to proceed smoothly to its next stage.

2.3   Land registration and legislative changes

2.3.1 Legal estates

Since 1 January 1926, there can be only two types of legal estate in land. These are:
- freehold: here the owner enjoys ownership and the benefit of occupying the property. He can dispose of these two rights at the same time by selling the freehold property with vacant possession;
- leasehold: here the term of years must be certain and it must be distinguished from a mere permission (that is, a licence). The tenant can either assign the interest for the period it has left to run or underlet and grant a shorter interest to a third party.

A freeholder can sell his right of ownership having leased away his right of occupation. This type of freehold is called a reversion. A reversion amounts to the expectation that the right of occupation will revert back to the freeholder when the period of the lease comes to an end.

From the above, it can be seen that in respect of one property, there can be a number of legal estates. This emphasises the importance of addressing one's attention to the type of legal estate one is being instructed to buy, sell or grant to a client.

In recent years, the Government's proposals regarding commonhold have gained growing support. Commonhold is not a new legal estate, but a special type of freehold ownership. The proposals contained in the Government's draft Bill envisage commonhold being an option for new and existing developments. A commonhold is made up of units, each with freehold title, but managed as one entity. The units as members of a commonhold association would own the freehold to the common parts of a development. The owners of the units would then have rights and obligations of and to other unit holders in connection with the land held by the commonhold association. If it becomes law, then the way residential and commercial developments are organised will be very different in the future. This is a development to watch over the next few years.

2.3.2 Legal interests

In order to enjoy one's land, it may be necessary to have limited rights over the property of another, and such rights are described as legal interests. Examples of legal interests are a right of way, a right of drainage or a right of a mortgagee.

A legal interest is different from a legal estate, since it includes neither a right of ownership nor a right of occupation. It must exist for a period equivalent to either a fee simple or a term of years absolute. Rights granted for a lesser term can only exist as a licence and, therefore, depend upon the personal relationship between the licensor and licensee for their enforcement.

A buyer of a legal estate for value is bound by all legal interests, whether or not he has notice of them.

2.3.3 Equitable interests

Broadly, these are interests in the land which are informally created or created for a period which is not equivalent to a legal estate.

The buyer for value is not bound by these interests unless he has notice of them and, where appropriate, they should be registered as a notice or caution on the register of title.

2.3.4 Overriding interests

Overriding interests are defined by s 70(1) of the Land Registration Act 1925. They are rights in favour of third parties and include rights of common, customary rights, public rights, rights of way, rights under local land charges, leases for any term not exceeding 21 years and rights of those in actual occupation of land. Overriding interests need to be watched extremely carefully by prospective purchasers and appropriate questions are contained in the Protocol documents to ascertain whether any such rights exist. Since these are not shown on the land or charge certificate, there is always the risk that one may purchase subject to them.

2.4   Joint ownership of land by individuals

Anyone can own a legal estate in land provided he is aged over 18 or over and not suffering from a serious disability which prevents him dealing with his affairs. The maximum number of co-owners of a legal estate is four.

It is important at this stage to distinguish between legal and beneficial ownership. Joint owners will hold the legal estate as joint tenants and each will be entitled to the whole unless the contrary is stated. With regard to the beneficial ownership, they may be entitled to a division of the proceeds either as joint tenants or tenants in common.

The distinction between joint tenants and tenants in common occurs on death. If one joint tenant dies, then the legal estate in the property passes to the other joint tenant. However, on the death of a tenant in common, his interest in the proceeds of sale passes under the will or intestacy rules as part of his estate.

Joint tenancy as to the beneficial interest is usual in personal relationships, such as between husband and wife. Tenancy in common is usual in business relationships.

Joint tenancy can be severed by one joint tenant serving written notice on the other or others. On service of such a notice, a tenancy in common in respect of the proceeds of sale is created.

Joint tenants have a legal right to call for the property to be sold so that each may take his specified share. The court might grant such an application where the original purpose for which the property was bought has ceased.

2.5   Corporate ownership

Companies can buy and sell property so long as they are empowered to do so by its Memorandum and Articles of Association in the same way as an individual. The contract is signed on behalf of the company by a duly authorised director or secretary and deeds are sealed with the company's own seal affixed pursuant to a resolution passed by the board of directors and attested by a director and the secretary or two directors.

When drafting the contract for a corporate seller, it is worth bearing in mind that the Unfair Terms in Consumer Contracts Regulations 1994 will apply if the purchaser is a private individual. These Regulations will apply to the sale of new building plots to individuals, as the property will be sold on a standard form contract. The effect of the Regulations is that unfair terms of the contract will be void, but the rest of the contract will remain binding on the parties. A term will be regarded as unfair if it creates a serious imbalance in the obligations between the parties to the detriment of the consumer. Similar guidelines apply here as are contained in the Unfair Contract Terms Act 1977. It is for the consumer to show that the terms are unfair, and that the consumer did not have the opportunity to negotiate the contract.

2.6 Conveyancing on behalf of the owner

It may be that a mortgagee exercises the power of sale conferred upon him where the borrower defaults on his repayments. Similarly, the owner of the land may become bankrupt and the land will vest in the trustee in bankruptcy who has the duty to sell for the benefit of the creditors.

In either of the above cases, the property can be sold, and a sale in such circumstances overrides most of the entries on the register. In the case of a mortgagee sale, any subsequent mortgages created will be overreached.

2.7 Land registration

The Law Commission and Land Registry have issued a joint consultative document entitled *Land Registration for the 21st Century*. The Land Registry are proposing to eliminate the 'registration gap' between the transfer and registration by means of a system of 'electronic conveyancing'.

As part of the Land Registry's move to 'electronic conveyancing', most titles recorded at the Land Registry have now been computerised, including the plans. Many practices now have online access to the Land Registry's computerised records using the system called 'Land Registry Direct'.

Land Registry Direct enables you to view the title registers of properties either by title number or address. You are also given the opportunity to print off copies of the registers. Unfortunately, the Land Registry has advised that the computerised register cannot be relied upon as a court document. In these circumstances, an application for office copy entries will continue for the time being.

The Land Registry are also developing the National Land Information Service (NLIS), which aims to provide electronic access to property information including the Land Registry and local authorities. Online access to local authority information would certainly assist in speeding up the conveyancing transaction.

From 1 April 2000, applications to the Land Registry for first registration or following the transfer of land will result in the purchase price being included on the Register. Since the Register is open to public inspection, anyone will be able to discover the stated price of a property transferred or registered after 1 April.

2.8   Legislative changes

Most of the legislative changes which have occurred will be referred to in the relevant chapters of this book. However, the Contracts (Rights of Third Parties) Act 1999, the Trusts of Land and Appointment of Trustees Act 1999 and the Trustee Delegation Act 1999 are of general effect, and it makes sense to mention them here.

2.8.1 The Contracts (Rights of Third Parties) Act 1999

This Act amends the doctrine that a person cannot enjoy the benefit of a contract unless he is a party to it. The Act gives certain non-contracting parties the right to enforce a contractual provision and applies to all contracts entered into after 11 May 2000. Under the Act, third parties can enforce rights expressly or impliedly conferred on a third party and contained in a contract. Currently, practitioners are dealing with this Act in a negative fashion by including exclusion wording in their legal documentation. We have included a form of wording that should ensure that the Act's effect is excluded from the contract:

> Unless it is expressly agreed that the Contracts (Rights of Third Parties) Act 1999 is to apply nothing in this Agreement will create rights in favour of anyone other than the parties to this Agreement.

In the future, the provisions of the Act may be used in the areas of collateral warranties in construction contracts and enforceable tenants covenants in multi-let buildings.

2.8.2 The Trusts of Land and Appointment of Trustees Act 1996

The Trusts of Land and Appointment of Trustees Act 1996, which came into force on 1 January 1997, made three important amendments to the property legislation. First, it abolished the statutory 'trust for sale'. It is now not possible to exclude the power to postpone sale and replace it with the new concept of a 'trust of land'. Express 'trusts for sale' can still be created, but the power to postpone sale cannot be excluded. This has meant associated changes to the court's powers. The courts, in exercising their powers relating to the trustee's exercise of his functions or declaring the extent of a person's interest under a trust, must have regard to the intentions of the person who set up the trust and the purpose for which the property is held. Secondly, the doctrine of conversion was abolished. This doctrine previously stated that equitable joint tenants or tenants in common are only interested in the proceeds of sale. Thirdly, it ensured that no new strict settlements could be created. However, existing strict settlements will continue as such.

2.8.3 The Trustee Delegation Act 1999

The Trustee Delegation Act 1999 came into force on 1 March 2000 and deals with the delegation of trustee functions by power of attorney. Prior to this Act, trustees were not permitted to delegate their functions using an ordinary power of attorney. The Act allows the delegation of trustee functions by ordinary power of attorney on enduring power of attorney, provided that, at the time when the act done under the power of attorney is done, the donor has a beneficial interest in the land's proceeds or income. When acting for a purchaser who is acquiring a property from a trustee's attorney acting under an ordinary power of attorney, the conveyancer must obtain a signed statement made by the attorney that, at the time of the act, the trustee had a beneficial interest in the property. If a trustee delegates his functions by ordinary power of attorney, he is liable for the acts or default of the attorney. If a trustee does not have a beneficial interest in the property then he must comply with s 25 of the Trustee Act 1925. The Trustee Delegation Act 1999 provides a prescribed form for the creation of such a power and specifies that commencement of the power is on the date the power is executed by the trustee. It is also now possible for a trustee to appoint his sole co-trustee as attorney; however, the role that capital monies must be paid to at least two trustees in order to give a good receipt still applies.

2.8.4 The Trustee Act 2000

The Trustee Act 2000, which came into force on 1 February 2001, made important changes. First, the Act creates a statutory duty of care applicable to trustees in exercising their functions. The Act states that a trustee must show 'skill and care as is reasonable in the circumstances of the case'. Secondly, the Act gives a trustee the power to make any kind of investment he could make if he was absolutely entitled to the assets in the trust. Thirdly, the Act provides a framework for collective delegation by trustees of their powers. It should be noted that individual delegation is dealt with under the Trustee Delegation Act 1999.

3 The Practice of Conveyancing: Freehold

3.1 Obtaining instructions

Most residential conveyancers will be provided by their principals with a loosely applied scale so that telephone quotations can be given. Some firms have close relationships with particular estate agents who are sometimes provided with a scale of charges which they quote on your behalf. In the last few years, many conveyancers have received instructions by email, either via their own websites or those of referral agencies. The practice varies.

Once the client confirms instructions, then a letter should be sent out detailing the fees and disbursements so as to avoid the possibility of any subsequent misunderstanding. In fact, new Practice Rule 15 states that such a letter should be provided. Practice Rule 15 also provides that the client should be told who will be conducting the work and the standards of service expected. Firms should have developed a precedent introductory letter in order to ensure that none of these matters are missed. Together with such a letter, it may be helpful to supply a step by step guide to the transaction, and an instruction form containing details of the client, property and marketing information. Often, fee-earners take instructions without obtaining building society account numbers or telephone numbers. This wastes time throughout the transaction itself.

The art of conveyancing depends as much upon a methodical assembly of information as it does upon knowledge of the law.

3.1.1 Facts to be obtained from the seller

- The client's full name (and what he or she prefers to be called), address, telephone number, fax number and email address.
- The address of the property being sold.
- The name and address of the estate agents.
- A description of the property being sold including its current use.
- Details of the buyer.
- The agreed sale price and a note of any additional items included in that price.
- Details of any conditions attaching to the sale, such as whether there is a time schedule which must be complied with or a dependent purchase. It is important from the outset that both seller and buyer are like minded about any envisaged time scale.
- The whereabouts of the title deeds. Without these it is not possible to prepare a draft contract. If the title deeds are not in the seller's possession and there is no mortgage, then they may have been deposited with the seller's bank or with another firm of solicitors. Where the property is mortgaged, the deeds will be deposited with the mortgagee and the account number should be obtained from the seller. The deeds to a property held by a mortgagee will be released subject to an undertaking given by the conveyancer that they will be returned to the mortgagee on demand or the mortgage will be redeemed. In those circumstances, when the lender chooses to be separately represented, the title deeds will not be released to the borrower's legal advisers, but copies supplied instead.

3.1.2 Facts to be obtained from the buyer

- The client's full name (and what he or she prefers to be called), address, telephone number, fax number and email address.
- The name and address of the seller and of the estate agents.
- Whether any preliminary deposit has been paid to the estate agents and, if so, how much. Payment of a preliminary deposit is merely a gesture of good faith, and does not constitute a binding contract.
- Address of the property together with a description of the property, its current use and its proposed use, and any peculiarities such as footpaths which go across it or tenancies to which it is subject.
- In whose name is the property to be vested? It should be noted that the maximum number of people in which the legal estate of a property can be vested is four.

- It is important that the buyer has considered how the purchase of the property is to be financed. Usually this will be by mortgage. Application for a mortgage advance from a building society requires a written application together with a payment of a valuation fee. After the property has been valued and the borrower's means checked, then if the building society is satisfied it will make an offer which, in some cases, requires express acceptance by the borrower. Instructions will also be sent to the legal advisers.

- The agreed price which may be apportioned as between the legal estate and the contents of the property. This is important to ascertain for stamp duty purposes.

- A target date for completion in general terms.

3.1.3 Lock out agreements

In recent years an interesting development in the conveyancing process has been the introduction of lock out agreements. This development is a reaction by buyers to the practice of 'gazumping', which has been prevalent in the property market.

Lock out agreements are common in commercial development work, but in recent times have been used in other areas of property work including the residential market.

Lock out agreements are designed to give a buyer a limited period of exclusivity within which to 'exchange contracts'.

If a seller breaches its obligations under a lock out agreement, then the buyer will have the remedy of damages or injunctive relief. It is worth remembering that injunctive relief will not extend beyond the exclusivity period. Damages focus upon wasted costs incurred by the buyer as a result of the seller's breach of the lock out agreement. The damages will not include any loss of profit which the buyer envisaged making. Both parties should ensure that the exclusivity period is certain. At the end of the exclusivity period, the potential buyer will have no further rights. The seller is free to dispose of the property as he wishes. In order to avoid breaching a lock out agreement, a seller who does not wish to sell to the other party to the agreement should wait for the exclusivity period to expire.

3.1.4 Assembly of information to send to a purchaser

Having taken instructions from the seller, his conveyancer must send a prospective purchaser a pre-contract package.

The pre-contract package includes the following:

- draft contract (in duplicate);
- evidence of the seller's title;
- seller's property information forms; and
- miscellaneous planning and guarantees relating to the property.

It has now been proposed that before putting a home on the market, the seller will be required to put together a standard pack of information for prospective purchasers. The seller's pack is to contain: title information; replies to standard pre-contract enquiries; search results and other local authority enquiries; copies of planning and listed building consents; the draft contract; any warranties and guarantees and a condition report. For leasehold properties, the pack should in addition include a copy of the lease, service charge accounts and the current insurance policy. Pilot projects using the 'seller's pack' have been conducted which appear to have reduced the period of time for an average conveyancing transaction. Currently, the 'seller's pack' is not compulsory, but it is a matter which all conveyancing practices should be preparing for.

3.2   Drafting the contract

The preparation of a draft contract consists of the information acquired directly from the seller or the estate agents together with the information contained in the deeds and documents of title.

For the purposes of residential freehold transactions, the draft contract should normally incorporate the *Standard Conditions of Sale* (3rd edn).

A conveyancer should read the *Standard Conditions*, a copy of which are contained in Chapter 14, as these govern the relationship of the buyer and the seller subject to any special conditions. Special conditions deal with those matters which are transaction-specific, and some popular special conditions are discussed later in this chapter. Conveyancers may produce their own precedent draft contracts.

We have set out below some guidance in filling out the contract contained in Chapter 14 which must be used if the parties are following the National Protocol:

- The agreement date is generally left blank until contracts are exchanged.
- The name and address of the seller and the name and address of the buyer.

- The address or a description of the property and a note as to whether the freehold or leasehold estate is being sold. If it is a sale of part of an estate, then the property description should refer to a plan. A suitable plan for use should be contained in the land or charge certificate. If the plan is out of date, then it may be necessary to ask the seller personally or through an agent to provide a plan. The plan can be referred to as for 'identification purposes only', which means that in the event of contradiction between the description and the plan, the description shall prevail. Alternatively, the plan can be referred to as 'more particularly delineated', which means that where there is a discrepancy, the plan prevails. It is a convention that the property will be shown edged in red on the plan. Rights benefiting the property do not need to be referred to, unless on a sale of part, new rights (for example, a right to lay conduits) are created.

- The title number of the property.

- The *Standard Conditions* provide that the seller sells the property free from encumbrances other than those that are referred to in the agreement or discoverable by inspection. Failure to disclose encumbrances may give the buyer the right to rescind the contract and claim damages. For this reason, full disclosure of defects and encumbrances is the best course of action. It is not necessary to disclose matters such as an existing mortgage which will be discharged on completion. Disclosable defects may be either third party rights such as an easement, covenant or lease, or defects in the documentary title. Any matters burdening the property should be set out in full, and a copy of the document providing details should be given to the purchaser. On a sale of part, it is common for new burdens to be placed upon the property and these should be specified here. If the property is being sold subject only to those matters on the charges register, then this is all that needs to be stated on the face of the contract. Where a number of encumbrances need to be included, then it may be easier to include them as a special condition.

- The seller should also provide the buyer with either a full or limited title guarantee. Standard condition 4.5.2 promises that the seller will transfer with full title guarantee. If the seller only wishes to transfer the property with 'limited' title guarantee, then the words 'full' should be deleted. When a seller sells a property with 'full title guarantee', then he impliedly gives the buyer the following covenants:

  (a) that the seller can dispose of the land as he purports to;

  (b) that he will at his own cost do all he can to transfer the title he has purported to give;

(c) that the property is transferred free from all encumbrances other than those the seller could not reasonably have known about.

A limited title guarantee is the same as a full title guarantee except that a seller of a limited title guarantee only covenants that he has not encumbered the property. He takes no responsibility for covenants created by his predecessors.

• The completion date should be inserted when contracts are exchanged, otherwise standard condition 6.1.1 provides that the completion date shall be 20 working days after the date of the contract.

• The contract rate clause is used to agree a rate of interest which is payable on late completion. The contract rate should be higher than the rate charged by banks for a bridging loan. Otherwise, a purchaser may not be encouraged to complete promptly, as it will be cheaper to complete late using a bridging loan. The Law Society rate contained in standard condition 1.1.1 will generally be acceptable for residential transactions.

• The price of the property being sold and the deposit clauses sometimes are left blank until exchange of contracts. It saves time having to retype the contract if the transaction does not proceed and the contract is required for an alternative buyer. The amounts stated here reflect the price of the land (including fixtures). Where a deposit is included, the *Standard Conditions* provide for this to be 10% of the price. However, a deposit of less than 10% may sometimes be agreed by negotiation between the parties' conveyancers and this negotiation usually takes place immediately before exchange of contracts. It may necessitate a further special condition in the contract. By virtue of standard condition 2.2, the deposit is paid on 'exchange of contracts' by the purchaser to the seller's solicitor who is to hold it as stakeholder. This means that the seller's solicitor holds the deposit as agent for both seller and purchaser. The deposit cannot be released to the seller until the contract is discharged. The deposit does constitute client's money and the seller is entitled to interest earned on the deposit money in accordance with the provisions of the Financial Services Act 1986. Standard condition 2.2 provides that if the seller is buying another property in a related transaction, he may use all or part of the deposit as a deposit in that transaction to be held in that transaction as stakeholder.

• A figure may be apportioned to the chattels if the price of the property is close to the stamp duty threshold. Remember that the deposit figure is based on the land value only. We refer you to Chapter 13.

3.2.1 Special conditions

If you read the back page of the contract in Chapter 14, you will see some suggested special conditions. Special condition 4 incorporates the Fixtures, Fittings and Contents Form in the contract. This will avoid any dispute regarding those matters which should remain with the property. Special condition 5 offers alternatives of either vacant possession or subject to existing tenancies. In the latter case, details should be supplied.

Other matters which may be special conditions are:

- the authorised use of the property for the purposes of current planning legislation;
- an attempt to avoid liability on the part of the seller for any representations given by him or on his behalf save for replies to enquiries given by the seller's solicitors, stating that the buyer proceeds entirely on the basis of his own survey and inspection. This is included to limit a buyer's claim for misrepresentation resulting from the seller's replies given in the preliminary enquiries;
- there may be positive covenants which the buyer is required to observe (for example, the buyer must erect and maintain a fence). These positive covenants should be included as a special condition and the buyer should be required to enter into an indemnity covenant in the Transfer in respect of the future observance thereof. The reason for an indemnity is that positive covenants do not automatically pass on each transaction and therefore the burden of these covenants needs to be handed down expressly to each subsequent buyer.

3.2.2 *Standard Commercial Property Conditions*

The *Standard Conditions* are drafted mainly for residential transactions. For the purposes of sales of commercial properties, the *Standard Commercial Property Conditions* (1st edn) should be used. A copy of these is reproduced in Chapter 14.

The *Standard Conditions* were drafted mainly for residential transactions and required substantial amendment if they were to be used for a commercial property transaction.

The *Standard Commercial Property Conditions* differ from the *Standard Conditions* as follows:

- The deposit must be paid by direct credit.
- The *Conditions* take into account the possibility of double insurance until completion and if payment under the buyer's policy is affected because of the insurance policy of the seller, the purchase price is reduced accordingly.
- If the property is subject to a lease then, on completion, the seller is to cancel his insurance policy and pay any premium refund to the buyer. The buyer is to hold the refund subject to the rights of the tenant. The aim is to protect the tenants against double insurance.
- Only the buyer can be required to pay compensation on late completion. Where both parties are in default, the seller cannot claim compensation for any period between contractual and actual completion if the seller himself is in default. If the property is the subject of a lease, then the seller can now elect to take compensation and the net income of the property.
- Apportionments. The day of completion is apportioned to the buyer. There are new provisions dealing with service charge where a property is subject to a lease with service charge provisions. Apportionment of service charge provides that on completion the buyer must pay the seller the amount of service charge incurred but not yet due from the tenant and the seller must account to the buyer for service charge payments received from the tenants but not yet incurred.
- Includes notice provisions for service by document exchange.
- If the property is leasehold, the *Conditions* provide a more workable mechanism for obtaining landlord's consent. Completion can be deferred for four months to allow for consent to be obtained. The *Conditions* also take account of the Landlord and Tenant (Covenants) Act 1995 by requiring the seller to enter into an Authorised Guarantee Agreement.

Special conditions which may be included for the purposes of a commercial transaction include:

- to make it explicitly clear that title deduction is to be prior to exchange of contracts;
- a jurisdiction clause;
- a surety covenant;
- sales of part;
- prohibition on sub-sales;
- provision for the agreed form of draft transfer to be annexed to the contract;

- provisions to deal with occupation pending completion;
- the seller to pay any refund of the insurance premium direct to an occupational tenant.

3.2.3 Sub-sales

Special considerations must be included within the contract if the transaction is to be a sub-sale.

The buyer must check that the contract does not have a restriction on sub-sales. The *Standard Conditions* do not restrict sub-sales of freehold land. The buyer must then enter into a contract with a third party prior to completion of his purchase.

The following special conditions may need to be inserted into the buyer's contract with the third party:

- The notice to complete must be for the same length of time as the notice in the contract between seller and buyer.
- Since the buyer is not the registered proprietor, he cannot deduce title to the third party. The third party must accept the title provided by the seller.
- The buyer, seller and third party must all be parties to the transfer document in order to transfer the legal and beneficial ownership of the property.
- If the amount payable by the third party exceeds the consideration due from the buyer to the seller, then the price must be apportioned in the transfer document between the seller and buyer and a receipt must be given by each.

Since the third party is dependent upon the buyer and seller's contract completing, it may be advisable for the third party to register its contract against the seller's title by either a notice or a caution.

3.3   Auction

Where the property is sold by auction, the contract will include particulars (the auctioneer's marketing document), conditions (usually the standard conditions supplemented by special conditions) and a memorandum (which is signed by both parties).

The following contractual provisions are specific to an auction:

- the contract must state a 'reserve price'. If not, the property will just be sold to the highest bidder;

- the seller may reserve its right to bid at the auction;
- the auctioneer's control over bidding, such as the right to refuse a bid and how to deal with bidding disputes;
- the amount (usually 10%) and method of payment of the deposit;
- whether the seller can withdraw from the auction; and
- the right to retract a bid should be excluded so that a contract is formed at the 'fall of the hammer'.

Under the *Standard Commercial Property Conditions*, the deposit is held by the auctioneer as agent for the seller rather than the stakeholder. The seller's conveyancer will also be expected to provide prospective bidders with the title documentation, copies of up to date searches and seller's property information forms in good time before an auction.

3.4   Side letters

It is important to remember that for side letters to be legally binding, there must be an offer, acceptance of that offer, consideration and an intention to create legal relations. In addition, if it is a side letter intending to vary a contract for an interest in land (rather than personal obligations between the parties), then it must comply with s 2 of the Law of Property (Miscellaneous Provisions) Act 1989. Section 2 provides that such a side letter must be in writing, incorporates all the terms that the parties have agreed (either in full or by reference to another document) and must be signed by each party.

3.5   Evidence of title

The seller should send to the buyer office copy entries of the property. Office copy entries are an up to date copy of the register entries. Office copy entries can be obtained either by telephone or on Form 109 from the District Land Registry for the area in which the land is situated.

Together with office copy entries should be any other documents of title which are referred to on the register and evidence of matters which do not appear on the register, but a purchaser would be subject to (for example, overriding interests – see Chapter 7).

The following points should be noted:
- If a seller has married since the date of the purchase, thereby changing her name, a certified copy of the marriage certificate should be included.

- Where one of two joint tenants has died since the date of purchase, a certified copy of the death certificate should appear.
- Where one of two tenants in common has died since the date of purchase, it may be necessary for the surviving tenant in common to appoint a new trustee for the purposes of the conveyance to give good receipt for the purchase moneys.
- Where a deed is executed by an agent, the seller's conveyancer should be given the original or a certified copy of the power of attorney.
- Where a tenant in common or the surviving owner or the sole owner of property dies, a certified copy of the grant of probate (if a will was made) or grant of letters of administration (if no will was made) should be supplied in order to verify the appointment of the personal representatives.

3.6   Pre-contract enquiries

For the purposes of residential transactions, the Property Information Forms which are part of the National Protocol scheme should be completed by the seller at the outset. Copies of the Forms are contained in Chapter 14. The Forms require the seller to tick the appropriate box and they provide the range of practical information which was previously contained in replies to preliminary enquiries.

The seller will deal with the Property Information Form Part I. Property Information Form Part II must be completed by the conveyancer and to some extent, the information sought from the Part II form double checks that given by the seller personally.

Also completed at this stage by the seller is the Fixtures, Fittings and Contents Form. Again, it is a simple question of ticking the relevant boxes. This Form is referred to in the contract and thereby incorporated.

All these forms must be submitted with the draft contract at the beginning of a residential transaction.

For the purposes of commercial transactions, the old form of preliminary enquiries is used. In order to speed up the transaction, the seller should provide the buyer with a copy of its standard form preliminary enquiries and replies.

3.7   Guarantees

With the title deeds and documents there may be various guarantees (such as timber or double glazing) relating to the property. The buyer must ensure that any guarantees are assigned to him on completion.

3.7.1 Buildmark

One of the most common and important guarantees that a conveyancer will come across is the National House Building Council (NHBC) Scheme (known as 'Buildmark').

The Buildmark scheme is divided into two parts. First, full cover is provided for two years against a wide variety of defects. If any defects arise, then the aggrieved buyer should first make a complaint to the builder in the hope that the builder will voluntarily put matters right. Should he fail to do so, or should he have gone out of business, the matter will be taken up formally by the NHBC, who will pay the compensation in an appropriate case.

The remaining eight years of the 10 year period are covered by a basic insurance against major structural defects.

NHBC will send the following documents to the house builder who registers a new home:

- an offer of cover – Form BM1;
- an acceptance – Form BM2; and
- the Buildmark booklet – Form BM3.

The first two documents, which are attached together, state the Buildmark number, the address of the home, and the name and membership number of the registered developer or registered house builder as the case may be. The documents all refer to this person as the builder. The booklet describes all the insurance benefits summarised in more detail than set out above. The builder should deliver these documents to the first buyer when contracts for the sale of the dwelling are exchanged.

By the offer of cover, the NHBC and the builder offer the first buyer of the home and all subsequent buyers protection set out in the Buildmark booklet. The term 'buyer' excludes developers or speculators who purchase the property for the purposes of resale.

The buyer should sign the acceptance and return it forthwith to the NHBC. Assuming all is well, the NHBC will send the buyer two copies of a 10 year notice (Form BM4). This notice confirms, amongst other things, that the home is within the scheme and it states the commencement date of the 10 year period and the maximum insured value. In the case of a flat or maisonette, the buyer will receive two copies of a common parts 10 year notice (Form BM5). The duplicate 10 year notice is intended for onward transmission to the buyer's mortgagee.

In recent years, other schemes similar to the NHBC scheme have been offered by certain large building companies.

3.7.2 Architect's certificate

For smaller builders, an architect's certificate replaces the Buildmark scheme.

An architect's certificate is issued to a builder at the completion of appropriate stages of building for the purpose of releasing stage payments from a purchaser.

A buyer requiring a mortgage will find it very difficult indeed to proceed with the purchase of a new property which possesses neither an NHBC nor an architect's certificate.

3.8 Planning

Planning matters are important, as a buyer will want to ensure that the property is being used in accordance with the law. The buyer's conveyancer will need to check that any planning conditions have been complied with and that the owner has not been served with notices to cease a particular use. In fact, in some property transactions it is the planning permission itself which gives the land any real value. When acting for the buyer you should, at the outset, check with your client their intended future uses for the property.

If building work has been carried out without a planning permission, then it is unlawful. However, if no notice of breach has been served within four years of the breach, then a certificate of lawfulness can be obtained. If the building work is in breach of a planning permission condition then, if no notice of breach has been served within 10 years of breach, a certificate can be obtained.

When acting for a purchaser of commercial property, the conveyancer must check that the current or anticipated use is lawful. If no planning permission exists and 10 years have passed from the unauthorised use without enforcement action being taken, then a certificate of lawfulness can be obtained. Express planning permission is not needed if the change of use is permitted by the General Permitted Development Order 1995. There is unlikely to be any doubt that residential use is lawful.

To flush out the issues early in the transaction, if the seller has planning permissions relating to the property, then these should be included in the pre-contract package. If the seller's property has been recently built or substantially altered, then the seller should have a copy of Building Regulations approval from the local authority and this should be provided as part of the pre-contract package.

3.9 Pre-exchange buyer's matters

After the buyer's conveyancer receives the pre-contract package from the seller, he must check its contents very carefully. In addition, he must ensure that the following matters are dealt with before exchange of contracts:

* finance;
* a survey; and
* searches.

3.9.1 Mortgage finance

In many property transactions, finance is required in order for the buyer to purchase the property. This will usually take the form of a bank or building society mortgage.

Sources of mortgage finance

Most estate agency firms now have their own financial advisor and, once a sale of a property is made, the in-house financial advisor will endeavour to put together a financial package with the appropriate building society and/or insurance company. Some firms of solicitors provide similar services. It is increasingly less common for proposed purchasers to approach banks or building societies direct, although established borrowers who are buying for a second or third time would be more likely to do so. It is the duty of the buyer's solicitor to ensure that contracts are not exchanged until after the mortgage offer has been received.

The maximum amount available to a buyer will depend upon his income and the value of the property. Institutions will generally provide a mortgage advance of three or four times the income of the borrower, but this might depend upon the prevailing interest rate and the borrower's other commitments.

Where a high percentage loan is made against the property a mortgage guarantee policy may be required, in respect of which, the single premium will commonly be deducted from the mortgage advance on completion. It is vital to read mortgage conditions carefully to see whether the lending institution proposes to make any deductions from the mortgage advance and to discuss this with the borrower carefully. Sometimes conditions attaching to an offer impose a penalty for early redemption. This should be drawn to the buyer's attention.

Mortgagees

One must ensure that the mortgage deed is completed properly and duly executed prior to the completion day. The borrower should understand the nature of mortgage lending and should recognise the meaning of some of the more important conditions attached to the mortgage advance. Generally, mortgage deeds are very briefly drawn, and there is a conditions booklet setting out conditions incorporated by reference.

The Law of Property Act 1925 confers important powers on mortgagees where there is default. Sometimes, these powers are improved or enhanced by the provisions of a mortgage deed.

Other conditions attaching to a mortgage offer generally relate to the condition of the property requiring an undertaking by a borrower to do certain work within a certain period of time after completion. Sometimes, a retention is made from the mortgage advance until stipulated works are finished. If the road in front of the property is not adopted at the time of completion, it is common for a small sum to be held back until either the production of a s 38 agreement or the road is formally adopted. Which is required will be clear from the mortgage conditions.

If the mortgage is an endowment mortgage, there will be one or more endowment policies which will either have to be assigned in favour of the mortgagee or deposited with the title deeds upon completion. Again, it is the duty of the borrower's conveyancer to check that such policies have been issued. Notice of deposit or assignment must be given to the insurance company after completion of the mortgage.

Types of mortgage

In an ordinary repayment scheme, the mortgage advance is repayable in full over the prescribed period, which is most commonly 20 or 25 years, and both the interest and the principal are repaid to the institution concerned. Initially, the major part of the repayment is interest and it is not until the later years that the capital is reduced significantly.

In an endowment mortgage scheme, the mortgage advance is coupled with an endowment policy to the full amount of the sum borrowed. On the basis that the policy is in existence, one merely repays interest to the institution lending the money at the same time as the premiums under a given policy. After the expiry of the given period, the sum of money which has accrued under the endowment policy should at least be sufficient to repay the principal to the lending institution and there should be an excess for the borrower. The overall cost of a endowment mortgage may be very similar to that of a repayment mortgage.

Sometimes, a repayment mortgage can be coupled with a mortgage protection policy. In such a case, a small monthly premium is paid to an insurance company so that, if the borrower dies before the end of the period of the mortgage, the amount borrowed is then paid off. This is automatically built into the endowment mortgage system.

The following are common mortgage conditions:

- If the borrower wishes to create a lease, he must consult his mortgagee and seek his permission.
- The most common system of enforcing rights against a defaulting borrower is the power of sale. The power is implied by virtue of ss 101–03 of the Law of Property Act 1925 and may additionally be expressed in the mortgage deed. The power arises as soon as the legal date for redemption has passed, which will be after the first few months of the mortgage advance. The power must have become exercisable and this will occur when:
  (a) the interest is two months in arrears;
  (b) there is a breach of a covenant in the mortgage deed other than the covenant to repay;
  (c) there is a failure to repay the loan, although three months' notice has been given.
- A mortgagor cannot prevent the sale after contracts have been exchanged. The mortgagor must act in good faith to obtain a proper price and apply the proceeds of sale in the prescribed way; any surplus must be held on trust for the mortgagee. Where a borrower is in difficulties, the major lenders may opt to lengthen the term rather than enforce their rights of sale.
- It is also possible for the mortgagee to appoint a receiver and to foreclose, but these powers are rarely exercised.
- The first mortgagee is protected by the deposit of the title deeds and this is sufficient to prevent dealings with the land without his consent. Second and subsequent mortgages are protected by the registration of a second charge certificate.

Mortgagee's instructions

It is of vital importance to read through the conditions attaching to the buyer's mortgage offer. Such conditions are now controlled by Practice

Rule 6, which provides a standard certificate of title. We refer you to Chapter 12 for more details.

Many clients do not understand the mortgage conditions. They may include important provisions such as requirements relating to insurance, a retention in respect of the defective condition of the property, early redemption penalties in respect of a fixed rate mortgage, requirements with regard to the production and inspection of endowment or other life insurance policies, an obligation to redeem existing borrowing prior to the completion of the mortgage, or an obligation to carry out certain stipulated works within a few months of the completion date. To overlook any of these conditions can have serious consequences for the conveyancer and can prevent completion from taking place. Careful analysis is therefore important prior to exchange of contracts and, in cases of uncertainty, you should telephone the bank or building society in order to discuss the provisions of the mortgage loan with them. It may well be necessary to seek a variation of the conditions or to seek confirmation that the conditions have already been met to the satisfaction of the mortgage lender.

Care must be exercised to ensure that a mortgage which has a time limit has not expired prior to the date anticipated for completion.

3.9.2 Surveys

The purchaser's conveyancer should advise his client to have a formal survey prior to exchange of contracts. The seller's conveyancer is very careful about answering any questions relating to the condition of the property and will generally qualify all the seller's comments about the structural condition of the property by stating that no warranty is given.

There are three categories of inspection that the property may receive. A mortgagee may only be concerned with a valuation of the property, and such valuations cannot be regarded as surveys. Better than a valuation, but not so thorough as a structural survey, is a 'home buyer's report'. A 'home buyer's report' represents a special form of survey which is not fully comprehensive, but deals with the most important aspects of the property's condition. It is less expensive than a structural survey and the terms of the report will be presented in a standard format containing a number of exclusion clauses. A structural survey is the most comprehensive inspection of a property which is possible.

Should the buyer have any complaints about the condition of the property after he has completed his purchase, then in the above cases, it will be the surveyor rather than the seller to whom he should look for a remedy.

3.9.3 Searches

The following searches will reveal further information about the property. Where speed of completing the transaction is of the essence, the seller's conveyancer will carry out the searches and give the results to the buyer at the outset. However, usually the buyer will conduct his own searches.

Land charges department search

The first search commonly undertaken at the outset of a transaction is a local search. There are two parts to this. First, there is Form LLC1, which is submitted in duplicate. This Form reveals the existence or otherwise of any local land charges (see Chapter 11).

When the Form is completed, it should either be despatched to the appropriate London borough council or, if outside London, to the appropriate district or borough council. They administer these searches, although they do not necessarily supply all the information themselves. The Form should be addressed to the Registrar of Local Land Charges.

The result of this part of the search will reveal such matters as:

- enforcement notices;
- whether the property is subject to outstanding conditions in respect of an improvement grant. These conditions generally prevail for a period of five years from the date that the improvement grant is registered and may, *inter alia*, prevent the seller selling to a non-owner/occupier;
- sometimes, a planning permission is subject to the provisions of what was commonly known as a s 52 agreement and is now called a s 106 agreement. These agreements are negotiated between the local authority and the developer and permit building works subject to the observation of a number of mutually agreed factors. These agreements are commonly registered as a local land charge and expressly draw the buyer's attention to its provisions.

The second part of the enquiries addressed to the local authority comprises a list of questions asked on Form Con 29.

The appropriate form is sent in duplicate to the district council or London borough council with the local land charges search referred to above. These now vary from one local authority to another, and you should enquire of each authority their current charge for dealing with Part I questions.

Part II contains certain further additional enquiries which will only be answered on payment of extra fees and if an express request is placed against each of those Part II questions. The first part of the search deals with standard enquiries that relate to all properties:

- Does the property abut a publicly maintained highway? If it does not, express rights of way are required, and the contents of the draft contract will need to be checked for rights of way. Such rights of way will normally be accompanied by maintenance obligations. The most thorough method of checking whether the property abuts a publicly maintained road is to colour on the plan the roads in the vicinity of the property and refer to that colouring in Box C of the form.

- Where a new property has been constructed on a development, the new road may not have been adopted at the date of undertaking the local search. In the absence of formal adoption by the relevant highway authority, one would expect to find what is commonly known as a 's 38 agreement'. This agreement is made pursuant to s 38 of the Highways Act 1980 and normally requires a new road to be made up to a specified standard and maintained for a year. The agreement may join in a bank or similar institution as guarantor. The developer will be required to make up the road to the necessary standard and, assuming all goes well, the road will be adopted without cost to the frontagers.

- Enquiry 5 will indicate whether or not the property has the benefit of mains drainage. An isolated rural property will probably have its own private drainage system. A new property on a development will eventually expect to drain into the mains drainage system and here, care is required. The adoption of the mains drains generally follows the adoption of the highway, but arrangements are different. Under s 18 of the Public Health Act 1936, the water authority can agree to adopt a private sewer or drain. The conveyancer must check the precise arrangements.

- There are a number of questions relating to planning matters. Question 7 deals with the existence or otherwise of a structure plan for the area. It is important to make it clear to one's client whether or not such a structure plan has been inspected, as this might affect the possibility of new buildings in the vicinity of the property or the alteration of existing arrangements of terms of use.

- Enquiry 16A asks whether there are any entries on the contamination register against the property. The new contaminated land regime which came into force on 1 April 2000 only deals with land that poses an unacceptable risk to human health or the environment. Entries on the register will reveal remediation notices and who should pay the 'clean up' costs. Enquiry 16A should, therefore, be checked very carefully, as these costs could become the responsibility of the buyer and could be enormous. Unfortunately, there is no procedure for land to be removed from the register following a 'clean up' operation. Therefore, if land is identified as contaminated and remediation has taken place, a prospective buyer should seek a letter from the local authority confirming that the property is no longer defined as contaminated. Although the principle behind the register is that the 'polluter pays', it is worth remembering that if the polluter cannot be found, then the owner or occupier of the land will be responsible for the costs of the clean up. When acting for a purchaser, if you have reason to believe that pollution may be present at the property, you must recommend that an environmental survey is carried out. If a purchaser wishes to press ahead with contaminated land, you should try to seek an indemnity from the seller or an insurance policy.

It is generally agreed that local authority search results are valid for three months. However, under TransAction, a search up to six months old may be validated under an insurance indemnity scheme.

Commons registration search

Such a search is important when dealing with conveyancing of vacant land. The search is made on Form CR21, which is dispatched to the relevant county council together with a fee of £6 and a plan. The point of such a search is that land the subject of the transaction may be registered by the local authority as having rights of common registered over it in favour of owners and occupiers of other properties in the vicinity pursuant to the Commons Registration Act 1965. There will be a register of those entitled together with the purposes of which they are entitled.

Coal mining searches

Such a search is important in those counties where coal mining either does or used to take place. Such properties may be subject to possible subsidence. The standard form of enquiry agreed by the Coal Authority and the Law Society should be used. Supplies of the forms and a directory which identifies those counties in which a search is appropriate is available from law stationers.

The fee required for such a search is £25 and the search is submitted to the Coal Authority. No coal mining enquiry would be required in respect of property in Bedfordshire, Buckinghamshire, Cambridgeshire, Cornwall, Devon, East Sussex, Essex, Greater London, Hampshire, Hertfordshire, Norfolk, Suffolk, West Sussex and Wiltshire. The standard form is intended for use in connection with domestic property and the enquiries relate to:

- past underground coal mining;
- present underground coal mining;
- future underground coal mining;
- shafts;
- surface geology;
- claims for subsidence damage;
- open cast for coal mining.

The standard form should be used in conjunction with a further form when dealing with non-domestic property.

Statutory undertakers' searches

These are searches of utility companies which can be made by a prospective buyer depending upon the property's location. They include enquiries of the following bodies:

- the Environment Agency;
- Railtrack;
- British Telecommunications plc;
- the Post Office;
- the Canals Authority;
- the Police.

An environmental search is particularly important when acting for a purchaser of commercial property. The cost of carrying out such a search is in the region of £40. Such a search will disclose past and present contaminating and polluting processes, landfill, waste treatment sites, nearby toxic substances, risk of subsidence and flooding. If the property does have environmental problems, it may prove difficult to sell, pose risks to health and environmental legislation provides that the purchaser could be liable for the clean-up costs.

The website home-envirosearch.com offers a useful free neighbourhood environmental search facility.

Such statutory undertaker searches are necessary when the property is of a great value and the speed of the transaction is not essential. Many of these bodies have powers of compulsory purchase and this is one of the main reasons for carrying out the searches. Details of the relevant bodies can be obtained from the Directory of Local Authorities.

3.10 Exchanging contracts

3.10.1 Acting for the buyer – when and how?

When satisfactory search results have been received and satisfactory replies have been given to additional enquiries arising from the information provided, the conveyancer is in a position to approve the draft contract and to return one part to the seller's solicitor for signature by the seller. At this stage, details of the price and the name and address of the buyer will be inserted and the contract can be sent to both parties for signature. It is important either to meet with the buyers in order to explain the information you have ascertained from the work done to date, or to send a written report to the buyers (this is preferable for future reference purposes). It is important carefully to explain to the buyer the precise nature of the property being purchased. Once this is done, the buyer's signature can be obtained to the contract and, at that stage, each party's conveyancer is likely to be in a position to exchange contracts, and this can be effected in a number of different ways.

Today, contracts are most frequently exchanged over the telephone in accordance with Law Society Formula A, B or C.

3.10.2 Acting for the seller – when and how?

When acting for the seller, the chief concern is to obtain the proceeds of the sale and to release the seller from any obligations he may have according to the title deeds. The contract should then be sent to the seller for signature.

3.10.3 Exchange of contracts

If there is a related purchase, the contract may be exchanged over the telephone and the conveyancers should agree a tentative date for completion with both parties and check that both parties are ready.

Where one conveyancer holds both contracts, Law Society Formula A is appropriate. Once ready to exchange, the conveyancer holding both parts agrees that he holds his client's part to the other's order from the time the exchange takes place, and that time is duly noted. They also agree that both contracts are dated with the date of exchange and the date for completion and the conveyancer holding the contracts undertakes to post his client's part by first class post to the other party that same day. Contracts are exchanged from that moment.

Under Law Society Formula B, both conveyancers hold their client's signed parts and, where appropriate, a cheque for the agreed deposit. Again, they speak on the telephone and agree to exchange with effect from a time that they both note. They both undertake to hold their client's part to the other's order and to post it by first class post that same day to the other and, where appropriate, this is accompanied with the deposit cheque. Contracts are exchanged from that moment. Whether using Formula A or B, it is common to synchronise exchange. This is done by one conveyancer at the beginning of a chain of transactions saying on the telephone that he 'releases' his client's part to the other so that he commits himself to exchanging contracts and provides the other conveyancer with the freedom to enter into a binding contract within a specific period of time. This system works well in practice, as many conveyancers have found it impossible simultaneously to exchange contracts on the telephone, thereby leaving a theoretical opportunity for one of the parties to change his mind in the few minutes it takes to ring him back.

Under Law Society Formula C, a chain of transactions may be exchanged over the telephone more satisfactorily. The conveyancer at the end of the chain is asked to release his contract for a specific period of time to the conveyancer acting for the buyer next in line. Precise details of times should be carefully recorded and each conveyancer should be available to speak to the other throughout the agreed duration of the release. Memoranda should be prepared accordingly. The conveyancer in whose favour the contract has been released is then free to undertake a telephone exchange of contracts in accordance with Law Society Formula A or B as appropriate, and can then return to the original solicitor at the end of the chain in order to complete the exchange of the released contract in the same way as he would if dealing with Law Society Formula A or B. Law Society Formula C, therefore, involves two phone calls, but there is an obligation to proceed by the conveyancer who agrees to release his contract from the moment he enters into that agreement.

There can be extremely serious consequences for failing to synchronise an exchange of contracts and it would be negligent conduct if one's client was to end up without a property or, alternatively, with two properties. For this reason, some firms insist on either senior or experienced personnel dealing with the act of exchange.

After contracts are exchanged, a completion date should be entered in one's diary, as should the date for making the necessary land registry search in order to ensure the completion date falls within the priority period of 30 days (see below).

It is important to obtain a redemption statement from the existing lender where acting for the seller and similarly, to request the estate agent's account, which is customarily settled by the conveyancer out of the proceeds of the sale on completion. It is probably better practice to have obtained a redemption statement prior to exchange of contracts in order to ensure that there is no negative equity. In recent years, negative equity has been an acute problem, most notably for those who do not intend to purchase again. Following exchange of contracts, the conveyancer will be required to give a professional undertaking to discharge the subsisting mortgage and clearly, such an undertaking cannot be fulfilled if the proceeds of sale are inadequate. It is important to inform one's client that exchange of contracts has taken place, and this can be done on the telephone followed by a letter. It is good practice to discuss the following matters with the client:

- assistance with regard to sorting out outgoings at the property (for example, Council Tax);
- the removal of the seller's fixtures and fittings, and checking the likely whereabouts of the keys; and
- reminding the client that the utility meters should be read on the completion date.

3.11 Raising requisitions on title

The standard form of these appears in Chapter 14. Additional questions may be asked, but they must relate to the title and must not duplicate previous questions. The standard form requisitions deal with the mechanics of completion. The standard form includes answers to the following:

- confirmation that replies to preliminary enquiries remain unchanged;
- confirmation that outgoings will be paid until the completion date and receipts will be produced. A supply of a completion statement indicating the balance required to complete;

- a list of the deeds and documents to be handed over on completion together with a further note of any deeds which may not be handed over and the reason why;

- confirmation that any outstanding borrowing is to be discharged on or before completion and, if it is not discharged before completion, an undertaking is requested to discharge the borrowing on the completion date and to forward to the buyer's solicitor a duly sealed Form DS1 as soon as possible. The type of suitable undertaking has been recommended by the Law Society, but the majority of conveyancers are content to accept an undertaking given in answers to requisitions which merely undertakes to repay the mortgage on completion and to remit the receipted mortgage deed as soon as it is returned to them by the mortgagee in question;

- confirmation that vacant possession will be given on completion and an enquiry as to the arrangements for handing over keys;

- whether there is any third party who should receive notice of the transaction. By and large, this relates to the sale of leases;

- what the arrangements are for completion, such as where completion will take place (most commonly today, through the post). Similarly, details of the seller's solicitor's bank account are requested. An enquiry as to the amount required from the seller's conveyancer on completion.

Additional requisitions which are raised may relate to defects in title, and the most common of these are as follows:

- unstamped or improperly stamped deeds;

- improperly signed deeds;

- deeds which refer to plans which are not there, plans which are not coloured or plans which are wrongly coloured;

- a misdescription of the property or the covenants or easements that go with it; and

- old mortgages in respect of which there is no evidence of discharge.

3.12 Drafting a transfer

The draft transfer is prepared by the buyer and approved by the seller. When the transfer is agreed, an engrossment is provided by the buyer. The intention of the transfer is to give legal effect to the terms of the contract.

The transfer will be in the form of either a TR1 (transfer of whole) or TP1 (transfer of part). Most firms will have standard precedents on the word processor.

Form TR1 is broken down into 13 boxes. Most of the boxes are self-explanatory. If you have additional information which does not go into any of the boxes numbered 1–11, then you should use Box 12. If you run out of space on Form TR1, then you can use the continuation sheets.

The transfer only needs to be executed by the buyer if he gives covenants to the seller or if there are co-buyers. The transfer includes a declaration whereby the co-buyers can declare whether the beneficial ownership of the property is held as joint tenants or tenants in common. However, the transfer must be executed by the seller and retained by him pending completion when it is dated.

When preparing a draft transfer, remember that it must be executed as a deed.

3.13 Making arrangements for completion

On completion, the seller's conveyancer must have in his possession a signed transfer, the deeds and documents of title, knowledge of the whereabouts of the keys to the property and a redemption statement in respect of any subsisting mortgage to be discharged. Generally, he will take the initiative and contact the buyer's conveyancer to ascertain that the CHAPS payment has been or is about to be effected. Once received, the keys will be released and the deeds and documents together with the duly executed transfer deed will be despatched by post to the buyer's solicitor. Simultaneously, he will discharge the subsisting mortgage and disburse the balance purchase moneys.

The buyer's conveyancer will have previously ensured that he is in possession of the mortgage advance on the date it is required and will proceed to organise a CHAPS payment to the seller's conveyancer's bank account for the balance required.

It is important that the buyer's conveyancer is in possession of clear results from the following pre-completion searches:

- Land Registry Form 94A (transfer of whole) or 94B (transfer of part). This search can be carried out by telephone. The 'search from' date should be the date that the office copy entries were issued. The purpose of a Land Registry search is to update the entries on the registers of title. The search also establishes a 30 working day priority period within which to register a dealing in the land.

- If the buyer is raising mortgage finance, it will be important to make a bankruptcy search against his name before completion. A search in the Land Charges Department, which is based in Plymouth, should be undertaken on a Form K16, and on that form it is only necessary to state the names to be searched. It is to be hoped that the land charges search result will reveal 'no subsisting entries'. Should further details be required, it is possible to make an application to the Land Charges Department for an office copy. There is a fee payable of £8 for each office copy. Searches may be undertaken by telephone or facsimile. Where possible, applications should be made by post unless application is urgent. The lender should be informed if any entries appear.

- A company search is done before completion where the seller is a company. The Companies Registration Office in Cardiff maintains up to date information from those companies who have supplied necessary information via their annual return or otherwise. Such information may not be disclosed by the result of a land charges search. The search result will reveal whether or not the company is in receivership or in liquidation and also, and more commonly, whether or not there are fixed or floating charges. Fixed charges should be redeemed before completion. If the company is a developer, it is likely that a deed of release will be handed over in respect of a particular property being sold so that the mortgage attaches, instead, to the retained properties. If there are only floating charges, these will not need to be redeemed, but it will be necessary to ensure that they have not 'crystallised'. A letter from the chargee will suffice.

Where the buyer's conveyancer is in receipt of the deeds and documents of title, he should check that these accord with the photocopies that he was previously sent. He should also check replies to requisitions to ensure that all additional matters have been cleared up.

3.13.1 Completion statements

In addition to the completion statement that the seller's conveyancer supplies to the buyer's conveyancer, it is also vital that each conveyancer provides a statement to his own client for checking. A precedent statement appears in Chapter 14, and the client should be requested to confirm his acceptance. An accompanying letter should seek consent of the client to pay estate agent's and legal fees.

3.13.2 Post-completion formalities

The seller's conveyancer

The seller's conveyancer will send Form DS1 (now being replaced by the ENDS system of electronic discharge) to the buyer's conveyancer as soon as it is returned from the mortgagee. The mortgagee will generally leave the date of the form blank, and the date should be inserted to coincide with the completion date. Once received, the buyer's conveyancer will release the seller's conveyancer from the undertaking given on completion.

The seller's conveyancer will generally pay the estate agents and, in so doing, ensure that account has been taken of any preliminary deposit. Where the mortgage which has been redeemed was an endowment mortgage, the seller's conveyancer will make certain that there is a deed of re-assignment in respect of the endowment policy and notice of re-assignment will be sent to the insurance company.

The buyer's conveyancer

The buyer's conveyancer will give notice of completion to the mortgagee if this is part of the particular mortgagee's procedural requirements.

The two key post-completion matters that a buyer's conveyancer must deal with are stamping and registration.

Stamping

Stamp duty is payable within 30 days of completion. For the rates of *ad valorem* duty at the time of writing, please see Chapter 13. The transfer will only have to be sent off to the appropriate office of the Inland Revenue together with Form Stamps L(A)451 if the transfer is for a consideration in excess of £60,000. See Chapter 14 for an example of a Form L(A)451.

Where stamp duty is payable, a cheque should be made in favour of the Inland Revenue and should accompany the transfer. The stamps form and a schedule are despatched together with any additional plan if needed of the property.

In those cases where stamp duty is not payable or the consideration is £60,000 or less, the stamping process is dealt with by the Land Registry simultaneously with the land registration process.

Registration

It is important to submit the application for land registration before the expiry of the protection period of 30 working days afforded by the Land Registry search result. This search should be renewed if this proves impossible.

The title deeds should be sent to the Land Registry together with a Form AP1 and registration fee. Form AP1 is provided in Chapter 14. The current registration fees are governed by the 1999 Fees Order.

Remember that if the buyer is a company, any charge must be registered with Companies House within 21 days of its creation.

Once the land registration process is completed and the certificate returned, it must be checked carefully. If it is a charge certificate, then once it has been checked, it must be lodged with the lender.

4 The Practice of Conveyancing: Leasehold

4.1 Facts to be obtained from the seller

Buying and selling leasehold property follows the same principles as enunciated in Chapter 3, but are slightly more involved. We have decided to point out only how a leasehold transaction varies from a freehold transaction.

If the seller instructs you to sell an existing lease, this will be described as an 'assignment'. If you are instructed to deal with the assignment of an existing lease, it is important to ascertain from the assignor (the seller) whether a premium is to be asked for from the proposed assignee (the buyer) and to establish from the terms of the lease whether the landlord's consent will be required.

Much of the above information can be ascertained from the seller by requesting him to complete the leasehold property information form in the same way as the property information form referred to in Chapter 3. We have provided you with a copy of the leasehold property information form in Chapter 14. This completed additional information form should be supplied with the original contract documentation to the buyer's conveyancer at the outset of the transaction.

4.1.1 Licence to assign a lease

It is the duty of the existing tenant desiring to sell his leasehold interest to the buyer to check from the terms of his lease whether or not the landlord's consent is required to the transaction. Generally, the landlord's consent is only required in respect of commercial leases where traditionally, the premises are let at an open market rent which is reviewed every three or five years. It is, therefore, of significance for the landlord to ascertain the means of the proposed assignee so as to satisfy himself that the assignee can afford to pay the rent that may now be payable and in the future may be required.

A lease which contains a prohibition against assignment will require the landlord to waive the covenant. If the seller fails to obtain consent to the assignment, then although the assignment may be valid, the buyer could face forfeiture proceedings for breach of covenant. Leases usually contain a qualified covenant against assignment. Such a covenant will state that the tenant may not assign the lease without the consent of the landlord. When such a qualified covenant is included, then a statutory proviso is added by s 19(1) of the Landlord and Tenant Act 1927 that such consent will not be unreasonably withheld. The tenant must still apply for the landlord's consent to the assignment and, if the landlord is acting reasonably, he can refuse consent. If the landlord reasonably refuses consent, there is nothing that the seller can do. However, if the landlord is unreasonably withholding consent, then the tenant can proceed with the assignment confident that the landlord cannot succeed with forfeiture proceedings. The problem for the buyer is that without landlord's consent or a court declaration that the landlord is being unreasonable, there is always the danger of a finding by a court that the landlord is reasonably withholding consent and that he may then bring forfeiture proceedings against the buyer. In considering whether a landlord is acting reasonably, useful guidance can be gleaned from the case of *International Drilling Fluids Ltd v Louisville Investments (Uxbridge) Ltd* (1986). In addition, the Landlord and Tenant Act 1988 places a duty on the landlord to give a decision regarding consent within a reasonable period of time and to give consent unless there are reasonable grounds for withholding it. Breach of this duty could lead to a claim for damages by the tenant.

Section 19(1A) of the Landlord and Tenant Act 1927 (as amended by the Landlord and Tenant (Covenants) Act 1995) provides that a lease of commercial premises can contain in its covenant against assignment conditions of the assignment which must be met. If the conditions are not met, the landlord can refuse consent whether or not he is acting reasonably. This section does not apply to sub-lettings.

If the landlord's permission is required, the tenant's conveyancers must ask the proposed assignee's conveyancer to produce references. A bank reference is always required and it is common for there to be a request for two further references, such as trading references or, where none are available, personal references.

Upon receipt of the references, these will be despatched to the landlord or the landlord's conveyancer. It is for them to decide whether or not they are satisfied with these references.

With regard to assignments of commercial leases, it is increasingly common practice for the landlord to insist upon a rent deposit deed whereby six or 12 months' rent must be deposited by the proposed tenant for the first or second year of the assignment, or to insist on a third party guarantee.

It is not uncommon for the landlord's conveyancer to make the landlord's consent conditional. For example, premises may be in a state of disrepair and agreement may be sought to put the premises back into repair before the licence to assign is finalised. Equally, it may be that there is a rent review due in the next few months and, in such a case, the new rent will be agreed at this juncture as part of the discussions which take place at the time of the licence to assign.

A licence to assign is merely a permission from the landlord to the existing tenant enabling him to sell his lease to a proposed assignee. Generally, the licence appears in the form of a deed, and this is carefully prepared by the landlord's conveyancer and submitted to the tenant's conveyancer, who in turn submits it to the proposed assignee's conveyancer for approval. The deed is drafted and submitted in duplicate. It is not uncommon for the deed to include a direct covenant as between the landlord and the proposed assignee that the proposed assignee will pay the rent agreed and observe all the conditions of the existing lease. Once the draft licence to assign has been approved by those concerned, it will be engrossed in duplicate with one copy described as the licence to assign and the other copy described as the counterpart licence to assign. The licence to assign is to be executed by the landlord, and the counterpart licence to assign will be executed by the proposed assignee. On completion, these two parts will be exchanged.

4.2   Pre-contract package

The seller's pre-contract package will contain the following:

- a copy of the lease;
- a draft contract (in duplicate);
- evidence of the seller's title;
- seller's leasehold property information forms;
- miscellaneous planning documents and guarantees.

4.3   Drafting the contract

This is the task of the seller's conveyancer where an existing lease is being assigned. The contract will generally be submitted in duplicate for approval together with a copy of the lease. Sometimes, a contract is dispensed with on the understanding that the matter remains 'subject to contract' until completion.

The preparation of the contract is the same as mentioned above, and below is a note of the differences in terms of preparation:

*   The description of the property should accord with the description contained in the lease and it should be expressly stated that the interest is sold leasehold.

*   The root of title will be the lease, and this contains the clauses and provisions which govern the entire transaction.

*   A further special condition will provide that the property is sold subject to the tenant's covenants in the lease in addition to the restrictive covenants and matters which may be contained in the freehold title which will, of course, bind the tenant even though he takes the leasehold title.

*   The requirement for the tenant to obtain the landlord's licence to assign may also be made a condition of the contract.

*   When acting for the buyer, a further special condition should be included so that the seller is obliged to produce copies of any superior landlord's and freehold title.

*   If the sale is not merely of the leasehold estate, but also of an existing business, the preparation of the contract will be fundamentally different in so far as it will additionally embrace the apportionment of the price as between the leasehold estate, the fixtures and fittings and the goodwill. It will also contain clauses dealing with the assignment of the goodwill and a clause restricting the vendor from competing within a certain radius for a certain period of time. There will be additional clauses relating to the existing staff, the continuation of the existing business by the seller up to completion, and the ownership and maintenance of the accounts, etc.

The following are the standard commercial property conditions which are relevant to a leasehold sale:

*   Landlord's consent. Completion must take place five working days after the seller notifies the buyer that the consent has been obtained or four months from the original completion date, whichever is earlier. There is a mutual right to rescind after that four month period

has expired. Neither party can object to a consent which is subject to conditions under s 19 of the Landlord and Covenant Act 1927.

- Express account is taken of the Landlord and Tenant (Covenants) Act 1995 so that the seller is obliged to enter into an Authorised Guarantee Agreement (AGA) if the lease requires it. An AGA is a document which is prepared on an assignment and provides that the tenant guarantees the performance of the covenants under the lease by the assignee.

As well as approving the draft contract, the buyer's conveyancer must consider the terms of the lease to be assigned. For details of the matters to look out for, we refer you to Chapter 5.

4.4   Evidence of title

If the term of the lease to be assigned is over 21 years, then the lease will be registered and the seller should provide office copy entries of its title together with a copy of the lease.

If the lease is unregistered, then title is deduced by the seller providing a copy of the lease and past assignments. If the assignment to the current seller took place more than 15 years ago, the seller need only produce that assignment. If the assignment to the current seller took place less than 15 years ago, then the seller would have to provide copies of previous assignments leading to the 15 year old root document.

Other than the above matters, unless the contract specifies to the contrary, the seller is not obliged to provide details of any superior leases and the freehold title.

4.5   Preliminary enquiries

As part of the pre-contract documentation, the seller shall provide the buyer with a completed leasehold property information form. Again, for the purposes of leasehold commercial transactions, the seller will prepare the old style preliminary enquiries. The buyer will be particularly interested in the following information that will be revealed by the leasehold property information forms or the leasehold preliminary enquiries.

4.5.1 Covenants

A complaint by the landlord may take the form of a notice under s 146 of the Law of Property Act 1925, which is generally required before a breach of a covenant or condition is enforced. No notice is needed where the rent or a sum reserved as rent is in arrears.

A covenant to decorate the premises in a particular calendar year imposes a duty at the beginning of that year and is not avoided because the lease is assigned before the end of it.

In most leases, there is an express covenant for quiet enjoyment, and where this is not expressly stated, it is implied. Similarly, there are implied repairing covenants by the landlord in residential tenancies granted for less than seven years. Additionally, the landlord will be expected to comply with any other covenants contained in the lease.

4.5.2 Service charges

In addition to the rent, leases of part of a building or of a unit on an estate will carry a 'service charge'. Service charge is a charge levied by the landlord for the maintenance of the building, its insurance and other outgoings which cannot be specifically attributed to one unit. The service charge accrues from day to day and, upon completion of the sale, is apportionable on a time basis. The seller will be required to state the date of the last payment, and attempts may have to be made to ascertain from the landlord the current charging rate. Service charges tend to vary from one year to another, and that depends on the overall cost of running the building or estate in which any given letting unit is located. A buyer should enquire as to whether the seller has exercised his right to obtain information from the landlord concerning the service charge. The tenant can request in writing from the landlord within one year after the end of the calendar year concerned a written summary of the costs affecting his service charge. The landlord is duty bound to comply with the request within one month, or six months after the end of the accounting year, whichever is the latest. This duty is enforceable by the local authority. A statutory right to information does not apply if the tenant is afforded reasonable facilities for inspecting certified accounts giving the same information, if there are no more than five flats in the building and if the tenant is afforded reasonable facilities for inspecting receipts and records. The local authority's housing association, tenants' associations and companies are exempt.

It will also be important to obtain details of the following:

- three years' service charge payments and copies of the accounts and invoices and certificates regarding payments;
- whether the service charge payments have been challenged;
- whether any substantial expenditure has been incurred or is contemplated which will lead to increases in the tenant's contribution.

4.5.3 Insurance

Where a lease contains a tenant's covenant to insure, and the landlord effects the policy, the tenant cannot rely upon the landlord continuing to insure. If the landlord is obliged to insure, ask to see a copy of the policy and ensure that the tenant's interest is subsequently endorsed on it, and ask to see an up to date schedule of insurance.

4.5.4 Dealing with a management company

Sometimes, a landlord of a block of flats or even a large Victorian house which has been divided into flats may not wish to retain the ongoing responsibility for the building after he has granted all the leases. In such cases, it is common for the leases granted to be for a period in excess of 99 years. In this case, leases will be sold for a considerable premium and will merely be subject to a small annual ground rent together with the annual service charges. Accordingly, the landlord's investment in the freehold reversion is very small indeed, and there is little advantage in him retaining the ongoing responsibility of the building. The landlord may, therefore, establish a management company, which will be a private limited company, in respect of which each new tenant will be required to obtain one or more shares. The purchase of these shares at a nominal price is likely to be made a special condition of the contract.

Each tenant of each flat will become a member of the management company, and they will agree among themselves as to who the directors and secretary should be. They will meet in order to decide matters of expenditure, the lighting and the heating of the common parts of the building, the decorating of passageways and the maintenance of any garden areas.

The management company will be required to comply with provisions of the Companies Act and, where tenants are unable to cope with this responsibility themselves, additional service charges will be incurred in seeking professional assistance.

Sometimes, the management company will have the freehold reversion transferred to it so that the management company additionally receives the ground rent. Arrangements may vary. Increasingly commonly, freehold interests are being transferred to the tenants.

4.5.5 Commercial premises

With regard to business premises, control and maintenance of the building generally remains in the hands of the landlord. Here, the leases are not granted for lengthy periods and 21 or 40 years would be the longest period in respect of which one would be expected to find a lease. These leases are not bought or sold for significant premiums and, as a consequence, an open market rent is charged which generally runs into thousands of pounds per annum. This rent is reviewed periodically in accordance with extensive provisions set out in a standard form of lease.

4.5.6 Raising requisitions on title

For residential conveyancers, the standard protocol form of requisitions will be used, but for commercial conveyancing the traditional form of requisitions will be used. Both are now being reproduced increasingly commonly by word processing packages, and particularly the large firms will adopt their own format. However, it is the information rather than the format which is significant to the buyer's conveyancer.

The seller is required to supply receipts for the outgoings and, in particular, the last receipt for rent and service charge paid to the landlord. The receipt is of significance, because it implies that there are no outstanding breaches of the tenant's covenants under the lease. The seller is requested to supply the name and address of the person who should be supplied with a notice of the transaction (usually the head landlord). Notice should be served within a stipulated period of time and in respect of which a small fee is likely to be required. This is the responsibility of the assignee's conveyancer, and the client pays the fee. Sometimes, a deed of covenant is needed between the assignee and the landlord.

As with a freehold property, there may be defects with the title. There may be a missing assignment or missing search results, or one of the assignments may not have been properly stamped by the Inland Revenue. If any of these or other eventualities occurs, additional requisitions should be raised so that there is a perfect title on completion.

Watch for a restriction in the proprietorship register which will need to be removed on completion by the landlord.

4.6 Drafting a transfer/deed of assignment

Where a lease is registered, Form TR1 will be filled out in exactly the same way as for a freehold disposal. We refer you to Chapter 3. However, it is worth remembering that if the lease is transferred with full or limited title guarantee, then this implies a covenant that the lease is subsisting and there is no breach of covenant making the lease liable for forfeiture. Wording should be included in the TR1 such as 'The property is sold subject to any subsisting breach of covenant relating to the physical state of the property which renders the lease liable for forfeiture'. Such a statement is contained in standard condition 3.2.2 and should be re-iterated in the Form TR1.

Where a lease is not registered, nor is it registrable (as in the case of short business leases), a deed of assignment may be prepared.

The following points should be noted:

- if a recital clause is included, it should recite the original lease together with any subsequent assignments;

- the description of the property in the parcels clause should accord with that contained within the lease, and it should be made clear that the leasehold estate is being transferred;

- the assignee should undertake to observe the covenants as appropriate, but there will be no need for an acknowledgment for production clause as the original lease and assignments would be handed over on completion. The sale of part of a leasehold property would amount to a sub-lease. In this respect, a new lease would have been prepared, thereby obviating the need for a deed of assignment.

The deed of assignment is prepared by the buyer's conveyancer and is submitted for approval by the seller's conveyancer. It is submitted in duplicate, and the engrossment is signed by the buyer and returned to the seller's conveyancer for signature by his client in readiness for completion. The deed of assignment or Form TR1 is dated on the day of completion.

4.7 Making arrangements for completion

The seller's conveyancer must check that he is in possession of the executed transfer or the deed of assignment duly executed by his client. He will then contact the buyer's conveyancer in order to set up arrangements for completion, which is likely to be through the post. They will previously have supplied a completion statement, which is more important when dealing with leaseholds, as it will include the apportionment of any rent and service charges.

The buyer's conveyancer will ensure that he has collected sufficient funds for completion and he will have previously sent his own statement to his client in order to collect the sums due.

In addition to any purchase price, he may have to pay an apportionment for rent and service charges. Rent is only payable in advance where it is expressly stated in the lease, otherwise the presumption is that it is paid in arrears. Appropriate arrangements will be made on completion, depending on the circumstances.

The buyer's conveyancer will also have to carry out the necessary pre-completion searches. If the lease is registered, then a Land Registry search should be undertaken. If the lease is unregistered, then land charges searches should be carried out against the seller, previous tenants and the superior landlords. In any event, if necessary, a company search should be carried out against the name of the seller.

4.8   Completion

On completion, the buyer of an unregistered lease will receive:
- the original lease;
- the original past assignments;
- the original deed of assignment executed by the seller;
- if necessary, the landlord's consent to the assignment;
- marked abstracts of the freehold and superior leases.

On completion, the buyer of a registered lease will receive:
- the original lease;
- the land certificate;
- the original TR1;
- if necessary, landlord's consent to the assignment;
- if the title is registered with good leasehold title, then the marked abstracts of the freehold title and superior leases.

If the leasehold estate is mortgaged, then the buyer will want either a receipt on the mortgage deed or a Form DS1 (soon to be replaced by the ENDS system). The buyer should also ask to see a receipt for the last rent due.

4.9   Post-completion formalities

Any stamping that is necessary will mirror the requirements set out in Chapter 3.

If the lease is unregistered, check whether there is a need for first registration.

If the transfer is of a registered lease, then there is the need to apply for registration of the transfer before the end of the priority period provided by the Land Registry search.

If there is a management company, then it will be necessary to register the transfer with that company.

Notice of the assignment or mortgage should be notified to the landlord's conveyancer and a registration fee paid. Failure to do so will frequently be a breach of covenant.

5 Grant of a Lease

5.1 Preliminary matters

The first matter to consider is whether the proposed lease relates to residential premises, business premises or an agricultural holding. It is essential to establish which of these three applies, because the law relating to each is fundamentally different and the style of preparing the lease is different. Most large firms of conveyancers possess precedent forms which can be used. If it is practical, it is often sensible to visit the premises in respect of which the lease is to be granted. This helps one to establish the rights that are required for the passage of services and mutual rights of support maintenance and rights of way.

The second point to consider is whether a full lease is necessary, or whether a tenancy agreement will be sufficient. In the case of a letting of three years or less, an agreement under hand only is permissible, and usually adequate. In general, use the simpler form of agreement under hand where this is applicable.

If the lease or tenancy to be granted is an underlease, ensure that its terms comply with those of the headlease and, in that case, it may well be convenient to provide for the periodic payment of rent in advance a few weeks earlier than rent is payable under the superior lease so that your client, the landlord, may receive that rent in time to pay out of it the rent reserved in the headlease.

When granting a lease, it is likely that the landlord and tenant will proceed directly to grant rather than including a contract.

A contract will usually only be included when there is to be a significant delay (for example, the premises have not been built, there needs to be a surrender of a lease at the premises, the landlord intends to develop the premises, planning permission is required or superior landlord's consent is required) to granting a lease and the parties want the certainty of knowing that when the delay is over, the parties must complete the lease.

5.2 Costs

Take instructions as to who is to pay the costs. From time immemorial, the tenant used to pay the landlord's costs of a lease, in the absence of specific agreement to the contrary; in the case of tenancy agreements, in the absence of any such agreement, the custom was for each party to pay their own costs, although this was often varied by agreement. Under the Costs of Lease Act 1958, each party to a lease or tenancy agreement bears their own costs, and their own costs only, in the absence of agreement in writing to the contrary.

When demand for rented property exceeds supply, landlords will seek to pass on their costs to tenants; but the Act is directed at what had come to be recognised as an anomaly; and departure from the Act can be resisted by a tenant. Nor is it a part of your professional duties (having advised your client of the legal position) to persuade a landlord client to seek to reverse the progress of law by written agreement to the contrary. But most landlords, especially the property owning companies, are well aware of the position and their power, and the purpose of the Act is more often honoured in the breach than the observance.

Only a conveyancer can charge for preparing a lease; whereas an estate agent or anyone else may, by law, prepare and charge for preparing a tenancy agreement of three years or less.

5.3 Evidence of title

If the lease is granted out of a freehold title, then unless the contract provides for it, the tenant is not entitled to see evidence of the freehold title.

If the lease is granted out of a leasehold interest (that is, it is a sub-lease), then the prospective sub-tenant is only entitled to see the leasehold interest out of which the sub-lease is being carved. There is no entitlement to see any superior leases or the freehold title.

The tenant should therefore ensure that deduction of the freehold title is a condition of the contract (see below).

5.4 Drafting the contract

Standard condition 8.2.4 provides that if the landlord is granting a term of over 21 years, then he must deduce title to enable the prospective tenant to register its interest at HM Land Registry.

The effect of a landlord including standard condition 8.2.4 in the draft contract is as follows:

- if the lease is granted out of a freehold title, then the landlord must supply the following:

  (a) if the freehold title is registered: office copy entries of the freehold title;

  (b) if the freehold title is unregistered: an epitome of title with a 15 year root;

- if the lease is granted out of a leasehold title (that is, it is a sub-lease), then the landlord must supply the following:

  (a) if the leasehold title is registered with absolute title: office copy entries; a copy of the lease from which the sub-lease is carved; and, if required, his mortgagee; and immediate landlord's consent. There is no need to examine the freehold interest, because HM Land Registry guarantees the leasehold title;

  (b) if the leasehold title is registered with good leasehold title or unregistered: office copy entries (registered leases) or past assignments (unregistered leases); a copy of the landlord's lease, if required, the consent of the landlord's mortgagee; evidence of the freehold title (if registered, then office copy entries or, if unregistered, an epitome of title with a good root of title 15 years from when the headlease was granted); copies of the superior leases; and evidence of each superior leasehold interest and the consents of the superior landlords.

When acting for the landlord, you must ensure that standard condition 8.2.4 is only included in a contract if the landlord has the evidence which is required. If not, then the standard condition must be amended or deleted.

Standard condition 8.2.3 provides that the agreed form of lease to be granted will be annexed to the contract.

When drafting a contract for the grant of a commercial lease, we would recommend that the *Standard Commercial Property Conditions* are used. We refer you to Chapter 4.

5.5   Drafting and reviewing the lease

Below are some of the main matters to consider when drafting or reviewing a lease.

5.5.1   Parcels (that is, description of the property)

If the letting is of the whole of the property owned by the landlord, it will, in general, be sufficient to state the address.

It often happens, however, that the owner is letting a part only of his property – a flat in a building, a cottage in the grounds of the landlord's house – so you need to be particularly clear and specific, often by reference to a plan. Note, particularly, the warning given by *Scarfe v Adams* [1981] 1 All ER 84. Every such case demands careful consideration to ensure: (a) that the tenant is granted all the rights that will be needed for the full enjoyment of the property let; and (b) that the landlord reserves all the rights that will be needed for the full enjoyment of the remaining property. Consider these requirements always under three headings, namely:

- rights of way giving access to and from the dominant or servient tenement;
- rights of water, gas, electricity, drainage, and any other services; and
- provision for the use, maintenance and repair of common structures, etc, such as a party wall, a shared bathroom and lavatory, the roof and main walls, a combined drain serving two or more tenements, the cleaning of a common hall and stairway, etc.

In many cases – particularly in lettings of flats and parts of a building – it is desirable that leases of all flats shall be on identical terms, otherwise it may be found, when seeking to enforce a right granted to one tenant, that in some respect it is unenforceable against another.

You will often best learn of these, and the provisions that need to be made, by talking discursively to your client of the nature of the premises and the letting. Consideration of a plan of the property may suggest provisions that have not occurred to either party; as may its inspection.

5.5.2   Fixtures and fittings

In the case of furnished lettings, all the contents will be specified in the lease, usually by reference to an inventory annexed to it, or signed by the parties. It is important from the viewpoint equally of landlord and tenant, that the condition of any article less than perfect should be stated in the inventory: otherwise there will be a dispute and possible loss for one party or the other if neither admits that they disembowelled the grand piano, leaving only the eviscerated container. In many unfurnished dwellings, it is also important to list fixtures and fittings included with the property. If not supplied by the landlord, if acting for the tenant ask for such a list, and, if it is not forthcoming, specify in a letter what your client declares them to be. Checking and agreeing the contents of the inventory at the commencement and end of the term is important. As above, it is also wise to take a deposit from the new tenant to be held against breakages and damages.

5.5.3 Rent reviews

It is established practice, in lettings for terms of more than five years, to provide for periodic rent reviews under which the rent payable for successive periods shall be either that paid during the previous period, or the market rent that the premises could command at the date of the review, whichever is the higher. When acting for landlords, advise them of the dangers of freezing a rent for too long a period without review.

Usually commercial leases provide for rent to be paid in advance on the usual quarter days (that is, 25 March, 24 June, 29 September and 25 December). It is also common for payment to be by direct debit or standing order.

5.5.4 Insurance

Make it perfectly clear in the lease who is to insure, and against what risks. If the tenant insures, provide that the insurance shall be in the full value of the property from time to time with a society to be approved by the landlord, and in the joint names of the tenant and the landlord. If the landlord is to insure, it is not uncommon to provide that the insurance premium which the tenant pays shall include three years' loss of rent and professional advisers' fees on any necessary repair or rebuilding. Comprehensive cover against fire and other risks, and 'index linked' cover, are common and desirable. If the property is located in London, consider insuring against terrorism.

In connection with insurance, it is also common and reasonable to provide that rent shall cease to be payable from the time that the premises may be destroyed by an insured risk.

In commercial leases, it is common for the landlord to insure the property and for the tenant to pay the premiums.

5.5.5 Outgoings

You will, of course, take specific instructions from your client as to who pays the outgoings. Be specific as to who bears the burden.

5.5.6 Repairs and decorations

The provisions in a lease on this subject are the most frequent cause of dispute between the parties, and the draftsman should therefore be most precise and specific on the subject. Whatever shall be excluded from the tenant's covenant should be included in a corresponding covenant by the landlord.

As to what is a reasonable division of liability for repairs, if you are asked to advise on the point, the general rule is that the shorter the term, the less the liability commonly fastened on the tenant. So, in a monthly letting, an agreement by the tenant 'to keep the premises in as good a state of internal decorative repair as the same are now in', perhaps excluding fair wear and tear, would be reasonable. In a short letting, it is also preferable for the tenant to have a schedule of condition of the premises prepared and have its repairing obligations limited to that schedule. In a letting of seven years or more, a full repairing lease might be appropriate.

When a part only of a larger building is let (as in the case of a flat or maisonette) it is reasonable for the landlord always to remain liable for the 'foundations, roofs, main walls and timbers', the common parts of the entire building and also for the decoration of the outside and common parts, and to give a covenant to that effect.

The full form of lease includes both a covenant by the tenants to carry out whatever may be their agreed share of the repairs, and a covenant to permit the landlord to inspect periodically, and to carry out any repairs of which the landlord gives notice to the tenants, and which the tenants then fail to execute. See that such a covenant provides that the tenants are only to do repairs 'for which they may be liable under their hereinbefore contained covenants', or similar phrasing, otherwise this second covenant may unintentionally impose a liability wider than this. Ensure, too, when acting for tenants, that the period provided for doing the repairs is adequate, as sometimes this is not the case. A reasonable form will provide that the repairs shall be commenced within a specified period, and thereafter proceeded with diligently.

Remember, and in a proper case advise your client of the implications of ss 11–16 of the Landlord and Tenant Act 1985 whereby, in lettings of dwellings since 24 November 1961 for terms of less than seven years, the landlord is responsible for the structure, for the outside, and for water, gas, electric, sanitary and heating installations. It is an obligation that, in general, the parties cannot contract out of these except so far as the tenants would be liable under their duty to use the premises in a tenant-like manner.

Always enquire (and this is of special importance when acting for tenants) as to the present state of the property, as to whether this is to be a covenant to put into a good and tenantable state of repair, and if so, whose responsibility that is to be. If, as commonly occurs, the point has not been considered or discussed between the parties, point out to prospective tenants that a covenant to keep in good repair 'and so to deliver up the premises at the end of the term' may involve their putting them into better condition than they are now in. The importance of this cannot be overemphasised, as horrible consequences can follow.

5.5.7 Assignment and sub-letting

All leases should contain some limitation on or prohibition of assignment or sub-letting. In the case of a short (monthly, quarterly or even sometimes longer) tenancy, an absolute prohibition is not unreasonable or unusual. For a longer lease, the most common provision is that a tenant may not assign without the landlord's consent, but provision is usually made that this consent shall not be unreasonably withheld. However, it is not unusual for there to be an absolute prohibition against dealings with a part (as distinct from the whole) of a property.

Always take specific instructions on the question of the right to assign from whichever party you act for. Remember that under s 19 of the Landlord and Tenant Act 1927, when a lease contains a covenant not to assign, etc, without consent, there is always implied, if it is not already in the clause, that such consent shall not be unreasonably withheld. However, this section does not apply when there is an absolute covenant against assignment, without any reference at all to consent. If acting for the tenant of commercial premises, be mindful of s 19(1A) of the Landlord and Tenant Act 1927 (as amended by the Landlord and Tenant (Covenants) Act 1995) and conditions on assignment. These conditions will not be subject to the test of reasonableness, so it is crucial they are considered very carefully at this stage. In general, in all but the shortest terms, tenants can fairly expect some right to assign, however qualified, even though, when you ask them, they say they have no intention of assigning, for neither they nor you can foresee what the future holds. So, in general, when you act for a tenant, seek a reasonable provision in this respect.

When the landlord is particularly concerned not to let to anyone not personally approved (as may be the case, for example, when the tenant of a part of the landlord's home will become a neighbour), provide that before sub-letting or assigning, the landlord is to have the option of accepting a surrender of the term. This will sometimes be a useful compromise.

In addition, when acting for a landlord, it is worth including a qualification to consent in the last five years of the term. This is important, because it is the tenant at the end who must leave the premises in repair and it is therefore important that he is solvent.

5.5.8 Alterations

The landlord will want to exert some control over alterations to the property to maintain the value of its reversion.

In commercial leases, it is common to see a clause prohibiting alterations without the landlord's consent. Section 19(2) states that the landlord's consent is not to be unreasonably withheld.

Part I of the Landlord and Tenant Act 1927 (as amended by Pt III of the Landlord and Tenant Act 1954) provides that the tenant can claim compensation from the landlord for certain improvements on the termination of the lease.

5.5.9 User

It is important to check that the user covenant is in accordance with the tenant's intended use of the property. Check with the tenant whether he has future plans which would mean a change of use. In addition, it is important to remember that many longer leases are marketable commodities and the wider the user clause, the easier it will be to dispose of it. Remember that if the lease contains a qualified covenant which allows the tenant to change the use of the premises with the landlord's consent, there is no statutory implied proviso that such consent will not be unreasonably withheld.

5.5.10 Landlord's covenants

Having reached the landlord's covenants, insert (on the principle of being explicit) appropriate covenants as to the repairs, insurance and outgoings, if any, for which the landlord is to be responsible, as well as the invariable covenant for quiet enjoyment and the proviso for cesser of rent in the event of damage or destruction by an insured risk. If the landlord is to insure, the lease should provide that he shall furnish the tenant with a copy of sufficient extracts from the policy and that the tenant will also be notified of any subsequent modification of or addition to the policy.

The covenant that should always be in the long leases – that, if required, the landlord will enforce covenants (such as not to disturb neighbours) in leases of other parts of a building – is equally appropriate in short term leases. So is a covenant by the landlord that all leases in the building shall be on similar terms.

Ensure that the tenant's and the landlord's covenants, taken together, cover the repair and maintenance of the whole of the premises let, including in the case of a flat the structure, roofs, foundations and common parts such as entrances, halls and stairs of the building, and any garden included in the letting or of which the tenant has use.

A landlord's covenant to repair does not include an obligation to 'rebuild', so if a wall, for example, collapses and complete rebuilding is required, this would not come within the scope of a covenant merely to keep in repair – so, when acting for a tenant (or a landlord for that matter), see that the missing word is included in the landlord's covenant.

5.5.11 Service charge

On a lease of part, the landlord seeks to recoup the maintenance costs of the whole building by a service charge. The tenant will repair its demise only and the landlord will repair the rest of the building and charge the tenant by the service charge.

The total cost of the service charge should be apportioned between the tenants.

In commercial leases, it is common for the tenant to pay the landlord's estimate of the service charge in advance and then, at the end of the year, overpayments and underpayments will be dealt with.

5.5.12 Forfeiture

It is usual to see the provision for the landlord to forfeit the lease on non-payment of rent or breach of covenant. If the tenant intends to mortgage the premises, you must check that the landlord does not have the right to forfeit the lease on the tenant's bankruptcy. Some lenders are not prepared to lend on leases which contain such a clause.

Most firms now have standard precedent leases which can be tailored to specific premises. If not, law stationers sell satisfactory printed form leases.

A lease sometimes contains an option for tenants, on giving notice within a prescribed period, to purchase their landlord's reversion to the lease, whether freehold or leasehold.

The tenant's interest should be protected by registration on the charges register by a notice that an option to purchase is contained in the lease.

An option to renew a lease must be registered in a similar manner if it is to bind a buyer of the reversion. An option to renew is regarded by the courts as a privilege. For it to be exercisable, the option should be expressed to depend on observance of the tenant's covenants, the tenant must have complied strictly with all the terms of the lease, and particularly with the covenants to pay rent and to decorate and repair.

It is easy to overlook the need to register an option in a lease: the item to this effect on your post completion agenda should serve as a reminder.

5.6   Notice to quit

Before serving a notice to quit for the landlord, ensure not only that it complies with the terms of the lease, but also that notice of any change of landlord has been given to the tenant. Once notice has been served, there is always a danger that, by subsequently accepting payment of rent, a landlord will have waived his notice and will have to start all over again should he wish to proceed. The danger is greatest when management is in the hands of agents, who may inadvertently accept rent. The danger may be avoided by adding to the notice to quit (the printed form of notice available at law stationers is recommended) the following notice:

> Take notice that without prejudice to this notice the Landlord will accept payments of rent from you only until this notice expires. After that date all payments will be accepted only as mesne profits for your use and occupation of the said premises and by accepting such payments the Landlord must not be considered to have waived this Notice to Quit or the Landlord's right to recover possession of the premises.

5.7   The duty of the tenant's conveyancer

It is the prime duty of the conveyancer acting for tenants to explain to them all the terms, and in particular any unusual ones, contained in the document. The operative word is 'explain'. It is not enough to gabble verbatim through the document to a stunned client. This duty was demonstrated by *Sykes v Midland Bank Executor and Trustee Co Ltd* [1970] 2 All ER 471, CA. In that case, a solicitor for the plaintiff undertenants, a firm of architects and surveyors, had failed to draw his client's attention to the effect of a clause prohibiting any user other than that of the plaintiff's business unless 'the permission in writing of the Landlord and Superior Landlord has first been obtained, such permission by the Landlord not to be unreasonably withheld'. The plaintiffs entered into the underlease on the mistaken belief that the superior landlord's consent could not be arbitrarily withheld, as in fact it was. The Court of Appeal held that the clause was unusual, that it might and did affect the plaintiff's interest, who should therefore have been warned of the possible arbitrary withholding of consent by the Superior Landlord to a change of use; and that the solicitor (or rather his estate, the defendants being his executors) was liable to the plaintiffs in negligence. In that particular case, the damages awarded were merely nominal (£2) because the court found that even if the clause had been fully explained, the plaintiffs would nevertheless have proceeded; but the warning light as to a conveyancer's duty is no less clear for that.

The case also decided that in the case of a partnership, it was sufficient for a solicitor to tender advice only to the partner dealing with the matter rather than all the partners.

In your own protection, it is desirable to have proof that you have explained the terms of the lease to the tenant; therefore, always mention in a letter that you want to see them for that purpose or confirming such an appointment. When there are unusual or onerous terms which your tenant client nevertheless accepts, record this, and the advice you have given them as to the possible effect of such terms, in a letter to them.

5.8   Pre-completion matters

The landlord will engross the lease in duplicate. The part to be executed by the landlord is known as the original lease, and that part which is executed by the tenant is known as the counterpart.

An important pre-completion matter for many short business leases is that an exclusion order is obtained. As part of the negotiations of a business lease, it will be established whether or not the tenant will be entitled to its rights of security of tenure. Sections 28–34 of the Landlord and Tenant Act 1954 provide a tenant of a business lease with the right at the end of the term of the lease to apply for another lease. It is these rights which many landlords seek to exclude in short business leases. In order to exclude the provisions of the 1954 Act, the landlord and tenant must jointly apply to a county court for these rights to be excluded. Provided the order is applied for correctly, the obtaining of the order should be a rubber stamping exercise by the county court. In order to obtain an exclusion order, the landlord will send to the agreed county court a claim form with lease annexed (in triplicate), a draft court order (in triplicate) and a court fee. For the purposes of speed, often conveyancers sign on behalf of their client the statement of truth contained in the claim form. This is a statement making it clear that both parties consent to the order being obtained. If a conveyancer signs on behalf of his client, he must ensure that his client has been made aware of the implications of the order and that he has his client's written authority.

On completion, each party dates their part of the lease and the leases are exchanged by post.

5.9   Post-completion

5.9.1   Stamping

The original lease must be stamped with *ad valorem* duty which is calculated on the amount of the premium and the rent payable. If the lease term is seven years or more, then the lease must also have a PD stamp. The counterpart lease must be stamped with a fixed £5 duty. For further details, please see Chapter 13.

5.9.2   Registration

If the landlord's title is unregistered, and the tenant is granted a lease for greater than 21 years, then it must be registered within two months of completion of the lease. If not, then title to the lease cannot be registered.

If the landlord's title is registered and the tenant is granted a lease of over 21 years, then it must be registered within the Land Registry priority period. In addition, the Land Registry will put a notice of the lease on the landlord's registered title. It should be agreed prior to completion that the landlord will put his title on deposit and provide the tenant with a deposit number.

5.10 Assured shorthold tenancies

The provisions of the Housing Act 1988 were intended to reverse the decline of rented housing and to improve its quality.

Most practitioners will appreciate that the first part of the objective has undoubtedly been achieved. Rarely a day goes by in the experience of many conveyancing practitioners without their being asked to organise a shorthold tenancy for a landlord, or peruse the contents of a draft agreement for a prospective tenant. In fact, the time has come when it is rare to be asked to organise a residential tenancy in any other form.

The concept of the 'assured' tenancy and 'shorthold' letting were first introduced by the Housing Act 1980. Some progress has been made in securing a greater element of contractual agreement between landlord and tenant.

An assured tenancy differs from a regulated tenancy in so far as the rent will be the market level rent agreed on a contractual basis between the landlord and the tenant as at the commencement of the tenancy. There is, in general, no subsequent recourse to a rent assessment committee on such an agreement.

Assured shorthold tenancies are for an agreed fixed term of not less than six months. The landlord has the right to vacant possession of the property at the end of the agreed term on service of notice. Should the tenant die before conclusion, there are no rights of succession under the assured shorthold tenancy.

If a tenant does not move out upon the date specified in the notice to quit, a landlord may regain possession of the property by the issue of the appropriate summons in the local county court without having to provide suitable alternative accommodation.

An assured shorthold tenancy can be for as long a period as the parties may agree between them. If it is mutually desired between both landlord and tenant that the period run beyond the contractual date, the landlord will not lose the entitlement to regain possession on the above terms, but may do so only on the conclusion of the next anniversary date. For example, an assured shorthold tenancy for 12 months may run on for a further 12 months without the need for the preparation of any additional documentation, but the landlord may bring the arrangement to an end only by the service of the appropriate notice two months before the conclusion of the second period of 12 months. Although the tenancy will effectively be converted to a periodic tenancy, the landlord does not acquire a secure tenant by allowing the term to run on.

The provisions of the Housing Act 1988 have not totally repealed the Rent Act 1977, but have amended and repealed certain of its provisions.

The provisions relating to assured shorthold tenancies came into force on 15 January 1989.

The 1988 Act is a weighty tome and the reader is referred to an annotation by Bowden, G, *Housing Act 1988,* 1989, Shaw and Sons.

In practice, the preparation of a shorthold tenancy agreement is very simple. Most conveyancers, and indeed many firms of estate agents, keep their own standard precedent, which is used with the necessary amendments as to parties, rent and the terms etc. It is usual to take a deposit against breakages or damage in the sum of one month's rent. This is repayable at the end of the term, as long as the property is returned in good condition.

The agreement must refer to s 20 of the Housing Act 1988 in order to enable possession to be recovered upon the expiry of the fixed term of the agreement. A minimum of two months' notice is required in order to bring the tenancy to an end in accordance with s 21. A simple notice is required in order to terminate any subsequent periodic tenancy arising.

The most important piece of advice we can give you is that, before tenants take possession, they must have received a standard form of notice informing them that the agreement is to be an assured shorthold tenancy. If this notice is not served on the tenants before the commencement of the term, the protection of an assured shorthold tenancy will not be available to the landlord. The notice is, therefore, a most vital document and is normally produced in duplicate with one copy being countersigned by the tenants in order to acknowledge safe receipt of the top copy. Both copies will clearly have to be signed by or on behalf of the landlord.

If there is a subsisting mortgage, the mortgage lender will require a similar notice to be signed by the new tenant agreeing to vacate if possessive proceedings are instituted. This notice is pursuant to Sched 2, Ground 2 of the Housing Act 1988.

Once the notice has been dealt with, and once the agreements have been signed (usually in duplicate), the tenants can go into possession and the shorthold tenancy begins.

As indicated above, many letting agents are now bypassing conveyancers altogether, and issuing their own standard forms that are often badly drawn and that omit any sensible provisions on the part of the landlord which might protect the tenants. It is curious how tenants' enthusiasm to be in the new property as fast as possible makes them so rash as to fail to take professional advice.

5.11 The role of letting agents

As market conditions have shifted from the sale and purchase of freehold residential property to the increasing popularity of rented residential property, many estate agents have set up departments to manage residential property. Such departments provide a comprehensive service to include finding tenants, vetting the tenants, making arrangements for inventories to be drawn and for the tenants to enter once the appropriate shorthold tenancy documentation has been dealt with.

Once the tenants are satisfactorily installed for their minimum period of six months, the letting agents will charge a weekly management fee and will collect the rent and deal with any other practical query that may arise from the tenant about the condition, the services, or the nature of the property.

Disputes do arise with letting agents. Sometimes, they fail to deal promptly with the tenants' requests. Sometimes, they misjudge a tenant and the rent falls into arrears. Sometimes, they fail to pass on the rent sufficiently speedily to the landlord's account. Occasionally, errors are made in the preparation of documentation at the outset. Solicitors are often requested to pick up the pieces if the relationship between the landlord and the letting agent comes to grief in one of the above ways.

Solicitors are usually involved for the purpose of serving a formal notice to quit upon a tenant who either fails to pay his rent or whose term is coming to an end. If a tenant does not respond to such a notice, county court possession proceedings may be necessary. A solicitor may also be requested to examine the conduct of the letting agents to ascertain whether there may have been any negligence in the conduct of their responsibilities.

6 Right to Buy: Conveyancing under the Housing Act 1985

The Housing Act (HA) 1985 provides for a new dimension to conveyancing. Council and some other tenants have the inalienable right of their own choice to buy the freehold or a long lease of their homes on favourable terms.

6.1 Who has the right to buy?

A secure tenant of a flat or a home occupied as the only or principal dwelling house which is owned by a local or other authority. The tenant must have been a secure tenant for not less than two years or for periods amounting together to not less than two years. A joint tenant who has occupied a dwelling house as his own principal home shall be treated as the secure tenant and, where the secure tenancy is a joint one, that condition need be satisfied only as to one of them.

If a local authority landlord disposes of his estate subject to an applicant's lease, the new reversioner is subject to the same obligations as the local authority (Housing and Planning Act 1986).

6.2 Acquisition from housing associations

Secure tenants have the right under the Act to purchase their houses from a private housing association, but not from a charitable one. The Act does not give tenants the right to buy their homes, but it allows them to buy another dwelling house and to be granted towards its purchase a discount appropriate to their housing association home. The procedure is somewhat complicated.

First, the housing association must be involved in the purchase and in the procession of the procedures which are, briefly, that the new home is bought in the name of the housing association who, in the same breath, transfer it to the tenant by sub-sale for the price paid for it, less the discount calculated on the previous home. Alternatively, the authority may take a shared ownership lease with the buyer. The authority does not itself have to investigate title, make searches, etc, but may leave this to the tenant's conveyancer; but the consent of the housing corporation must be obtained and tenants should never commit themselves to a purchase until both the housing association and the housing corporation have agreed the terms of the transaction. The wisest course is to make the housing association a party to the agreement to purchase.

6.2.1 The price

The price for a freehold or leasehold dwelling house is its value on the open market with vacant possession. For the grant of a lease, it is assumed that the seller is granting a lease of 125 years at a ground rent not exceeding £10 per annum. In both cases, the sale is with the same rights and subject to the same burdens as are specified in the Act (s 127).

6.2.2 The discount

A person exercising the right to buy is entitled to a discount calculated as follows:

- if the period to be taken into account is less than three years, 32%; and

- if that period is three years or more, 32% plus 1% for each complete year by which the period exceeds two years, but not together exceeding 60% (s 129 of the HA 1985), or 70% for a flat (Housing and Planning Act 1986). But, the discount must not be such that the price would be less than the cost to the council in the previous eight years (Housing Act 1988).

If the right is exercised by joint tenants, the section shall be construed as if the one whose substitution would procure the largest discount were the secure tenant (s 129(3) of the HA 1985).

6.3   Resale

If the dwelling house is sold, or a lease granted exceeding 21 years, otherwise than at a market rent, within three years, the discount or a proportion thereof must be repaid; but the amount to be repaid is reduced by one-third of the discount for each complete year that has elapsed between the dates of completion of the purchase and the resale (Housing and Planning Act 1986). There are various exemptions when the buyer is a relation or the disposal is compulsory.

The discount provisions are entered as a charge at the time of first registration of the buyer's acquisition.

6.4   The right to a mortgage

A buyer has the right to a mortgage from the selling authority towards the purchase.

The amount that secure tenants, exercising the right to a mortgage, are entitled to leave on mortgage, or to have advanced to them, is the aggregate of:

- the purchase price;
- such costs of the landlord or the housing corporation as are chargeable to the tenant under s 178, which entitles the landlord or, as the case may be, the housing corporation, to charge the costs incurred in connection with the mortgage; and
- any costs incurred by the tenant and defrayed on the tenant's behalf by the landlord or the housing corporation (s 133).

Procedure in the case of a local authority mortgage is somewhat simplified compared with a building society or other mortgagee – there will be no special conditions of advance common in building society mortgages and, although title may be deduced to the mortgage department of the council, there will normally be no requisitions. The council will directly collect the mortgage advance, giving credit for this on the completion statement. The legal department of the council will attend to all formalities of completion such as stamping and denoting documents, registering title, etc. To this extent, therefore, the work of a buyer's conveyancer is greatly reduced.

6.5   The machinery of purchase

Tenants claiming the right to buy either freehold or leasehold must serve on their landlord a written notice claiming that right – the form must be obtained from the landlord.

The landlord must, within four weeks (within eight weeks if the period counting towards the three years includes a period when the present landlord was not the tenant's landlord), serve on the tenants a notice either (a) admitting, or (b) denying the tenants' right to buy, stating reasons if the right is denied (s 144).

When the secure tenant's claim to exercise the right to buy has been established, the landlord must serve on them, as soon as practicable, a notice describing the dwelling house, stating the price at which, in the opinion of the landlord, they are entitled to the freehold or leasehold interest, and the provisions that the landlord considers should be incorporated in the transfer or grant (s 125(1)–(3)). This notice follows a valuation of the property by the district valuer for the authority.

The landlord's notice must be accompanied by a form of notice to be used by the tenants if they require a mortgage.

6.6   Common provisions in the purchase documents

The transfer or grant shall not exclude or restrict the general words implied under s 62 of the Law of Property Act 1925 (Sched 6, Pt I, para 1 of the HA 1985). The transfer or grant shall include all such easements and rights over the property, so far as the landlord is capable of granting them, as will put the buyer in a position similar to that which he was in under the tenancy. The transfer shall also contain such easements and rights for the benefit of other property as were available against the tenant under the former tenancy.

In practice, both drafts and engrossments of transfers and leases are prepared by the landlord. Schedule 6, Pt II lays down provisions to be in the transfer of freeholds.

A transfer shall not exclude or restrict the 'all estate clause' implied under s 63 of the Law of Property Act 1925. Section 63 provides that every conveyance validly passes all rights and interests on the property conveyed.

The transfer shall be for an estate in fee simple subject (but otherwise free from encumbrances to: (a) the tenant's encumbrances; and (b) the burdens in respect of the upkeep or regulation for the benefit of any locality of any land, building, structure, works, ways or watercourse. The transfer shall be expressed to be made by the landlord as beneficial owner. By virtue of the schedule, there shall be implied the following covenants by the landlord:

- to keep in repair the structure and exterior of the dwelling house and of the building in which it is situated;
- to keep in repair any other property over or in respect of which the tenant has any rights by virtue of the schedule; and
- to ensure, so far as is practicable, that any services to be provided by the landlord and to which the tenant (alone or with others) may be entitled are maintained at a reasonable level and to keep in repair any installation connected with the provision of those services (Sched 6, Pt III, para 14).

Note that there are some clauses that a tenant would normally require, such as a covenant by the landlord to enforce covenants by the other tenants of other flats, that are included in the statutory lease.

6.7 Completion

When a secure tenant's claim to the right to buy has been established, the landlord is bound as soon as all matters relating to the grant and mortgage have been agreed or determined (s 140). Completion is normally by bank draft sent through the post – most local authorities have no facilities for completion by credit transfer.

If tenants fail to complete, the landlord can serve on them a notice requiring them to complete.

7 Registered Land

7.1 First registration

The registered system of conveyancing governs most of the transactions which take place in England and Wales.

The following transactions will mean that a property must be registered at the appropriate Land Registry:

- transfer of freehold land whether by way of sale or gift;
- assignment whether by sale or gift of a lease which at the date of the assignment has over 21 years to run;
- a grant of a lease for over 21 years;
- an assent of a freehold title;
- an assent of a leasehold title that has over 21 years to run;
- a mortgage of a freehold title; and
- a mortgage of a leasehold title that has over 21 years to run.

The above dispositions must be registered within two months of completion, otherwise the transfer will be void.

It is also worth remembering that you can apply for voluntary first registration.

7.2 Land charge certificates

There is a central land register which records the ownership of land in England and Wales. It is the process of registration which is the crux of this system. Failure to register prevents the legal estate from passing.

Registration is performed by a number of district land registries, each being responsible for certain counties. Upon application being made to them, they will issue a certificate to the proprietor of the land or mortgagee and this will replace the old title deeds. The certificate is legal proof of title and is guaranteed by the State. Where there is no mortgage, it will be described as a land certificate and where there is a mortgage, it will be described as a charge certificate. If there is more than one mortgage, each mortgagee will have its own certificate. If a mortgage applies to more than one property, then a charge certificate supplement will be issued in respect of each property. The charge will be contained in a separate cover (the charge certificate).

The certificate will be returned by the Land Registry together with a notice of completion of the registration and at that stage the certificate should be carefully checked for spelling mistakes or other matters which appear to be incorrect. If there are errors, these will be put right by the Land Registry quickly without charge.

7.2.1 The certificate and its registers

The certificate is correct as of the date it is issued. The date is contained on the certificate itself. Subsequently, the certificate may become out of date, so that the central registry records are different from the actual certificate. Copies of the recent applications and changes may be applied for either by undertaking a land registry search (Form 94A, for £4) or by requesting office copy entries (Form 109, for £8). The certificate itself is divided up into three registers.

The property register contains the title number, type of estate (freehold or leasehold) and the description of the land by reference to the filed plan, which is based on the ordnance survey and its postal address. It also contains easements such as a right of way or right of drainage and exceptions and reservations. Easements, exceptions and reservations, declarations and other similar matters may not be set out in full in the property register, but may be referred to by reference to a deed or document which has been incorporated with the certificate generally at the back. This is particularly common practice when dealing with the sale of property on a housing estate. If the title is leasehold, the property register will also provide brief details of the lease.

The proprietorship register sets out the type of title (see below), together with the name and address of the registered proprietor. Any restrictions on the right of the registered proprietor to deal with the property freely or to receive the proceeds of sale will also be set out, preceded by the words 'Notice' or 'Caution'.

The following are the types of title:

- Absolute freehold title is the best title. The registered proprietor is the owner of the fee simple subject only to encumbrances protected by an entry on the register, overriding interests and interests of beneficiaries if the proprietor holds the land as a trustee. These should not cause a problem, as the purchaser can overreach them.

- Absolute leasehold title is subject to the same matters as absolute freehold title, but also subject to the covenants and obligations of the lease. The Registrar can only be given absolute leasehold title if the Registrar knows that the landlord has the power to grant the lease. The Registrar will need to have examined evidence of any superior leases and the freehold interest.

- Good leasehold title is the same as absolute leasehold title except that the Registrar cannot guarantee that the lease is valid.

- Qualified freehold/leasehold title is when the Registrar may find a flaw in the title and a qualification can be put on the title with the owner's consent. If consent is not given, the Registrar will grant possessory title only. Qualified title could be granted where a transaction was carried out in breach of trust and registration is subject to the beneficiaries.

- Possessory freehold/leasehold title will be given when the Registrar is not satisfied with the evidence of ownership. This may be because the applicant's title is based on squatter's rights or the title deeds have been lost. It means that the registered proprietor's ownership is subject to all pre-registration claims.

It is possible to upgrade a class of title if further evidence of title becomes available. In the case of possessory title, this can be upgraded to absolute freehold or leasehold title if title has been registered for at least 12 years and the Registry is satisfied that the proprietor is in occupation.

The charges register includes burdens on the title such as restrictive covenants, easements benefiting adjoining or neighbouring land, leases for a term greater than 21 years and registered charges such as mortgages.

7.3   Other interests

In addition to those matters which are contained in the registers of the certificate, a buyer takes subject to minor and overriding interests. It is important to remember that these interests are not mutually exclusive.

7.3.1 Minor interests

Minor interests are, in fact, mainly what would be described as equitable interests in unregistered conveyancing. They can be split into three categories: registrable dealings which are not yet registrable; equitable interests behind a trust; and other matters. Other matters include restrictive covenants, equitable leases, easements, contracts for sale and options.

Unlike an overriding interest which, as its name suggests, overrides the certificate, a minor interest is only binding if it is entered on a register. If acting for a buyer and there are no protective entries on the register, one need have no qualms; if there are, one will, of course, question them by requisition or otherwise.

If acting for the owner of a minor interest and protection is required, this will be by registration of a notice, caution, restriction or (rarely) inhibition. One of the commonest and most important is a contract for the buyer of a property protected by a notice. It is not common practice to register notice of a contract, but when there is an unusually long deferred completion date, or when your buyer client suspects the good faith of the seller, or if there is a contract by correspondence, or for any other special reason peculiar to the particular transaction, a notice should be seriously considered and the client consulted and advised.

7.3.2 Notices, inhibitions, cautions and restrictions

Notice

Notices may be entered on the charges register of title to protect 'minor' interests, for example, an estate contract, a grant of easements over registered land, a lease or agreement for a lease which is not an overriding interest and other matters which all persons dealing with the land should receive notice of.

The application to register is on Form AP1, which must be accompanied by the document creating the interest and a certified copy or examined abstract thereof. The land certificate should also be deposited at the Registry, which means that the consent of the registered proprietor is needed before a notice can be registered. If there is a registered charge, the charge certificate is needed if the chargee is to be bound.

The notice procedure ensures that if the notice is valid, then any buyer takes subject to it.

Inhibition

Bankruptcy of a registered proprietor is protected by a bankruptcy inhibition and is put on the register when the receiving order is made.

Caution

The registration of a notice is a friendly proceeding carried out, in general, with the co-operation of the registered proprietor. When that person is unwilling to be party to the application, however, there is a hostile procedure available by the caution against dealings. This is made on Form CT2, signed by the cautioner or his conveyancer and accompanied by a statutory declaration (printed on the same form). The interest protected must be such that the court will enforce against the land or charge, and the cautioner must be a person interested in any land or charge registered in the name of another person.

Examples of interests that can be so protected are the following:

- beneficial owner in fee simple;
- person beneficially entitled to the lease referred to;
- purchaser under a contract for sale;
- claimant in an action in the Chancery Division of the High Court of Justice;
- equitable mortgagee under a memorandum of charge.

A further example is the registration of either a notice or a caution to give priority to a charge and bridge the gap between its creation and registration.

The effect of registering a caution against dealing is that no dealing will be registered without the cautioner's consent or until the expiration of a 'warning off' notice (14 working days) served on the cautioner by the Chief Land Registrar. Within the period of the notice, the cautioner must withdraw or justify the claim.

Restriction

Last amongst these devices for the protection of interests in registered land is a restriction on the powers of registered proprietors to deal with their land; for example, that partnership property shall not be disposed of after the death of one of the partners without the consent of his personal representatives; or that no disposition is to be registered without the consent of the chargee (this last one is not an uncommon precaution of building societies). A restriction ensures that the registered proprietor complies with any necessary provisions before a disposition takes place.

Application to register a restriction must be made on Form 75 signed by the applicant or the applicant's solicitor; the land or charge certificate must (in all but exceptional circumstances) accompany the application. This means that the consent of the registered proprietor is needed before a restriction can be registered.

As to interests not requiring protection by noting on the register, see below.

7.3.3 Overriding interests

Overriding interests are the Achilles' heel of registered land conveyancing, whose 'practical object ... is to confer certainty' (Ruoff, TBF and Roper, RB, *The Law and Practice of Registered Conveyancing,* looseleaf edn, London: Sweet and Maxwell, May 2000, 6-01). But, not all the skills and ingenuity of the law draftsman could wholly circumvent the deviousness of ancient land law. By s 70(1) of the Land Registration Act 1925:

> All registered land shall ... be deemed to be subject to such of the following overriding interests as may be for the time being subsisting in reference thereto.

The following list of these interests contains some which are not of frequent significance for the conveyancer, or will be covered by the searches described in Chapter 3. The complete list is printed inside the cover of every certificate, and the most common are easements, rights acquired under the Limitation Act 1980 (squatters' rights), local land charges, rights of persons in actual occupation, leases for any term not exceeding 21 years granted at a rent without taking a fine, etc (see s 70(1)(a)–(k)).

But, it is s 70(1)(g) that is the nightmare of conveyancers:

> The rights of every person in actual occupation of the land or in receipt of the rents and profits thereof save where enquiry is made of such person and the rights are not disclosed.

> This is intended to deal with persons who may have acquired an interest in a property. Occupation protects this interest. Persons who are in occupation but have not acquired an interest cannot claim an overriding interest.

So, how do buyers ensure that they will not, as they walk into their new home, be saddled with an unwanted bedfellow (to mix a couple of metaphors!)? There is no other register they can search, as in the case, for example, of local land charges for unregistered land. It is little consolation for the frustrated buyer that the seller has contracted to give vacant possession of the whole property: a successful claim for damages may not be your client's idea of a happy home, so enquiry and inspection of a property must always be made.

There is really no absolute guarantee of security. The preliminary enquiry of a seller as to what other persons occupy the property is one precaution. It is wise, when the seller has a spouse, to have him or her execute the contract, even when the other spouse is absent from the property. A notice on the register gives notice of a prior claim under the Matrimonial Homes Act 1983. With all this, and with conveyancers, if not always their clients, being professionally responsible, the chance of disaster is really extremely rare.

8 Boundaries

Determining the extent of a property's boundaries is the responsibility of the buyer. Unless excluded from the contract, standard condition 4.3.1 shall apply, which provides that the seller shall not be obliged to define precisely the position or ownership of the boundaries. Provided that the boundaries were clear on first registration, ownership of the boundaries will be shown by a letter 'T' on the filed plan. The 'T' should be to the side of the boundary line of the person who owns the property. This clearly establishes ownership of the boundaries. However, the actual position of the boundaries cannot be relied upon from the filed plan. In establishing the extent of the boundary, it may prove useful to look at pre-registration title deeds and ordnance survey maps, and to use various common law rebuttable presumptions.

If discrepancies arise between the physical boundary and the title plan, then a buyer should include a special condition in the contract requiring the seller to offer a statutory declaration to the Land Registry in respect of any additional land.

There have been two particularly important pieces of legislation dealing with boundaries in recent years: the Party Wall Act 1996 and the Access to Neighbouring Land Act 1992.

8.1 Party Wall Act 1996

The following are the key provisions in the Party Wall Act 1996:

- An owner and adjoining owner may agree to build a new party structure which straddles the boundary and agree how the expense of the structure is to be shared. The adjoining owner can refuse to consent to the works, and then the owner may only build on his land with the foundations projecting under the adjoining owner's land. Any dispute must be resolved in accordance with the Act.

- An owner has wide powers to deal with an existing party structure including the rights to underpin, thicken, demolish, repair and reduce the height of party structures. Any dispute must be resolved in accordance with the Act.

- An owner has the right to excavate and construct a structure within 3–6 m of the adjoining owner's building. Any dispute must be resolved in accordance with the Act.

- Before any of the works above may be started, the owner must serve notice on the adjoining owner setting out what is proposed. The timing of the notice is very important. In the case of party wall work, at least two months' notice must be given, while only one month is required for excavations for foundations. Time is not an issue if the adjoining owner agrees in writing to the works. In the case of all notices, if the adjoining owner fails to respond within 14 days, they are deemed to have dissented and a dispute has arisen. The adjoining owner can serve a counter-notice setting out conditions for the works to be carried out. An owner must comply with a counter-notice unless this would injure him or cause unnecessary expense or delay. If the owner does not consent to a counter-notice within 14 days, then a dispute arises.

- The Act contains the following general provisions:

  (a) the owner must not cause unnecessary inconvenience to any adjoining owner;

  (b) the owner shall compensate the adjoining owner for loss or damage as a result of his work;

  (c) where the owner lays open part of the adjoining owner's land/building, the owner must erect proper hoardings or shoring protection;

  (d) all works must comply with statutory requirements;

  (e) all works must be in accordance with agreed plans;

  (f) the owner and his agent have rights of entry onto the land of the adjoining owner to execute works;

  (g) the cost of the works are apportioned according to the use that the owner and adjoining owner respectively make of the structure;

  (h) refusal/hindrance by an adjoining owner who is entitled to access is a criminal offence; and

  (i) funds must be put aside as security where either owner is concerned that the other may not meet its debts.

- When a dispute arises under the Act, then it is dealt with by a surveyor(s) appointed jointly by the owner and adjoining owner. Costs are in the award of the surveyor(s). There is a right of appeal to the county court within 14 days of the award.

8.2 Access to Neighbouring Land Act 1992

This piece of legislation provides that:

- the applicant need not be the owner;
- the works must be necessary for the preservation of the whole or part of the dominant land which cannot be carried out or which would be substantially more difficult to carry out without the necessary entry;
- the right relates to basic preservation works: it does not extend to improvements or development work unless incidental or consequential to preservation works;
- the Act does not permit the granting of a permanent easement;
- the dominant land (benefiting from the right) can be commercial or residential: if commercial, as well as discretionary compensation being awarded to the owner of the servient land, the court can order the payment of a premium;
- application is made to the county court for an access order. If an access order is granted, it is registrable and binding on successors in title of the respondent. The court must refuse to grant an access order where it is satisfied that the respondent would suffer unreasonable interference with his land. It is not possible to contract out of the Act;
- the benefit of an access order will not pass to successors in title to the dominant land;
- the applicant can be required to provide security for financial liability and insurance.

9 Time Limits

Stipulations by the *Standard Conditions of Sale* (3rd edn) and *Standard Commercial Property Conditions* (1st edn):

- Unless fixed by the contract, the completion date is 20 working days after the date of the contract, but time is not of the essence of the contract unless a notice to complete has been served.

- If the money due on completion is received after 2.00 pm, completion is to be treated as taking place on the next working day, and this means that interest at the contract rate is payable on the outstanding purchase money.

- In apportioning any sum, it is assumed that the seller owns the property until the end of the day from which the apportionment is made and that the sum accrues daily at the rate at which it is payable on that day. This commonly relates to the Council Tax or water rates. In the *Commercial Conditions*, the day of completion is apportioned to the buyer.

- It is assumed that such outgoings accrue at an equal daily rate throughout the year and, where any sums to be apportioned are not known on the actual completion day, apportionment is to be made according to the best estimate available. As soon after completion as the amount is known, a final apportionment is to be made and notified to the other party, and any resulting balance paid no more than 10 working days later.

- The contract provides a timetable for the dealing with evidence of title and preparation of the transfer deed. The seller must send the buyer evidence of the title immediately after making the contract. The buyer may raise written requisitions six working days after either the date of the contract or the day of delivery of the seller's evidence of title on which the requisitions are raised, whichever is the later. The seller is to reply in writing to requisitions raised four working days after receiving them. The buyer may make written observations on the seller's replies within three working days after receiving the replies. The buyer's right to raise requisitions or make observations is lost after the expiration of the relevant time period. With regard to the transfer deed, the buyer is to send the seller a draft transfer at least 12 working days before the completion date. The seller is to approve or revise that draft and either return it or retain it for use as the actual transfer within four working days after the delivery of the draft. If the draft is returned, the buyer is to send an engrossment to the seller at least five working days before the completion date. The periods of time in respect of dealing with the title and in respect of dealing with the transfer deed may run concurrently. If the period between the date of the contract and completion is less than 15 working days, the time limits are reduced by the same proportion as that period bears to the period of 15 working days. Fractions of a working day are to be rounded down, except that the time limit to perform any step is not to be less than one working day.

• Where a party is unable to complete on the appropriate day, condition 6.6 provides that a notice to complete should be served upon the defaulting party and 10 working days is afforded by this condition within which period completion must be effected. If not, legal action of breach of contract can be instituted, and the position here is set out by standard conditions 7.5 and 7.6.

• A more ample exposition of the standard conditions of sale is set out by Silverman, F, *Standard Conditions of Sale: A Conveyancer's Guide*, 6th edn, 1999, Tolley.

9.1 Durability of search results

9.1.1 Local land charges search

The result of a local land charges search is treated as valid for a period of three months after the date of the search result. However, to remove the problems associated with the length of time upon which the result of a local search can be relied, the Law Society has arranged an insurance policy to be used in the case of any residential property where the purchase price does not exceed £500,000 and where the date of exchange of contracts is not more than six months from the date of the result of the most recent search on the property. The insurance covers the buyer and the buyer's lender. It provides indemnity for the difference in the market value of the property at the time of exchange of contracts caused by an adverse entry arising between the date of the result of the earlier search and the date of exchange of contracts. The cover is up to the limit of indemnity under the insurance policy which is limited to the purchase price of the property.

9.2 Stamping

Application for stamping a document must be made within 30 days of the date of the document. A delay beyond that period may incur the payment of additional duty known as penalty duty.

9.3 Application to the Land Registry to register the transfer of the legal estate

The time limit applicable to such applications depends on whether application is for first registration of for a registration of dealing. First registration must be applied for within two months of the date of completion, otherwise the legal estate will not pass to the buyer. In the case of dealing with registered land, the application must be sent to the registry within 30 working days of the search result in order to obtain the priority conferred by that result.

10 Fees

10.1 Local land charges search/local authority search

There is no standard local authority search fee. It is, therefore, important to ask each authority what they charge for Part I of a local authority search. An average fee at the time of writing would be £75 plus £5 per question in respect of each of the Part II matters on the search form.

Where it is appropriate to ask questions in Part II of the local authority search, the necessary boxes should be crossed and an additional fee per question should be despatched. Care should be taken with regard to the Part II questions. For example, if your client is purchasing a substantial property with some acres attaching to it, it is vital that you ask the public footpath question.

It is possible to ask questions which are not either in Part I or Part II of the local search form. If you propose to ask the local authority to answer such questions, you should ask them what they will charge for providing an answer.

A personal search is available at some local authorities. Again, the arrangements vary. An urban authority which deals with its own highway matters can probably provide an unsigned search result on the same day, although the cost of this may well be about £10. If a search is required on a tight timescale and you cannot carry it out personally, then there are companies which offer the service for approximately £150 and can fax you the results. Make sure that the search company you employ carries adequate indemnity insurance and that the search result is acceptable to the buyer's mortgage lender.

10.2 A commons registration search

A commons registration search costs £6 which is payable to the appropriate county council.

10.3 Application for office copy entries

An application for an office copy entry of the register including a filed plan costs £8 per copy.

The registration, renewal, rectification or cancellation of an entry in the register is £8 per name and the certificate is also £8 per name.

10.4 Company searches

Company searches are generally conducted by using the services of a law stationer and charges will depend on the extent of the search required. A conveyancing company search stops short of a full search of the register and the approximate cost will be £25 per company. Before making such a search, check with the stationer whom you are requesting to do the work.

It is possible to obtain limited free company information online using the website of the registrar of companies at www.companieshouse.open.gov.org. In addition, if you are a larger conveyancing firm, you may consider paying for online access of the whole register.

10.5 Land registry applications

Keep the latest Land Registration Fee Order in the office. At the time of writing, the latest Fee Order is 1999. If in doubt as to a fee, telephone land registry enquiries on 0845 308 4545.

Land registration fees were significantly simplified by the two scales introduced by the 1996 Fee Order. Scale 1 applies to first registration and dealings for value. Scale 2 applies to, *inter alia*, voluntary transfers and mortgages.

Credit account facilities offered to solicitors for payment of land registry fees are a convenience in more ways than one. A credit account avoids errors and saves time. Apply for facilities to the Accounts Section, HM Land Registry, Burrington Way, Plymouth, PL5 3LP.

11 Common Problems

11.1 Local authority search result

It is important to check the search results received and, where there are entries which are not acceptable, the transaction should not continue until adequate explanations have been obtained. Common problems arising from the results of local authority searches include the following:

- An enforcement notice registered against the property. This will indicate that there either is or has been an unauthorised use of the property which was not voluntarily discontinued. It is important to check to what the enforcement notice relates, whether it is now being complied with and whether the authorised use accords with the client buyer's requirement.

- An improvement grant. It is increasingly common for older properties to be renovated with the benefit of an improvement grant from the local authority. Full details of the improvement grant are required because these are registered as a land charge and carry conditions which affect the property for a period of five years after the date of registration of the grant. Improvement grants are made pursuant to the Housing Act 1985 and the relevant conditions must be carefully scrutinised to ensure that the transaction envisaged is authorised and will not result in an obligation to repay the amount of the grant. If such an obligation is imposed, it is important that the seller is required to discharge it.

- Section 106 agreement (formerly known as a s 52 agreement). Such an agreement was made pursuant to a planning permission in respect of the property. It will contain conditions and it is important to obtain a copy of the agreement and confirmation from the seller that the conditions imposed have been fully observed.

- The listing of buildings. It may be that the property has been listed within a particular category by the Department of the Environment as being of special architectural interest. Such a listing does not necessarily detract from the property, but depending upon which category of listing applies, it can prevent significant alteration to the overall appearance of the property.

- The property may be situated in a conservation area or smoke-control zone under the Clean Air Act 1956. Neither of these revelations is dramatic, but again, they affect the freedom of the buyer to enjoy the property.

- The property may not abut a publicly maintained highway. The variable situations which can arise in this regard have previously been discussed, and the implication as far as services to the property are concerned should be considered.

- The revelation of planning permission refusals, copies of which have not been sent with replies to the property information form. The buyer's conveyancer should require the seller's conveyancer to obtain such copies. The last planning permission is important, as earlier permissions may have been superseded. Copy refusals are also important, because these might be of relevance to the buyer in his future intentions for the property.

- The existence or otherwise of a structure plan by the relevant local government authority and its stage of preparation. Many clients are acutely concerned with their environment and they assume that, at the date of buying the property, proposals for development for land in the vicinity will be revealed. This is not necessarily the case, and the client buyer should be notified accordingly. If he requires further enquiries to be made, these should be carried out at the local authority as well as asking the seller whether he knows of any proposals for local development.

- Public drainage. The local authority search might reveal the absence of a public drainage system and, in such a case, the buyer's conveyancer must ascertain whether the property has the benefit of any drainage system. If it is a private drainage system, further enquiries should be raised as set out before.

- Some local authorities now maintain a contaminated land register. It is important to ensure that the property you are purchasing is not adversely affected but that, if it is, appropriate enquiries are made to ensure the structural adequacy of the property.

11.2 Pre-contractual information

Many sellers' conveyancers encourage guarded replies to pre-contractual information. Upon receipt of this information, the forms should be carefully analysed and those enquiries that have been unsatisfactorily answered or which lead to other potential questions or problems should be raised again, with a view to obtaining a more precise response. Particular matters to be looked for are:

- Boundaries. It is important that the client buyer should acquire what he thinks he is getting and that the seller should have authority to sell it. Sometimes, plans are inaccurate and boundaries have been moved. Sometimes, there are ongoing disputes concerning boundaries. The ownership of boundaries may be unclear and boundaries may be dilapidated or even non-existent. The first task of a buyer's conveyancer is to check that the boundaries are precise and accurate and that, if they have been moved, this was in agreement with the neighbours and the deeds accurately reflect the current ownership of the seller. This is particularly important when dealing with the conveyancing of a rural property.

- If the buyer is acquiring a property which is less than 10 years old in respect of which there is no NHBC guarantee certificate, a further enquiry should be made as to the status of the builder and whether or not architect's certificates were supplied at the time of construction. Architect's certificates are sufficient to vouch for the good construction of a property and should be obtained by small builders who are not registered with NHBC. If neither exists, the buyer should be advised to have a very thorough survey of the property. This is the only remaining option.

- The seller's conveyancer may draw a distinction between those services which are 'connected' and those services which are 'available'. The difference between the two is obvious, but if the buyer has a gas oven and, on completion, discovers that the gas main is located some 20 yards away from the property, there could be some adverse consequences for the buyer's conveyancer if this fact has not been pointed out to the buyer before contracts are exchanged. It is important to ascertain whether the services cross over neighbouring property and, if so, by what right.

- The authorised use of the property should be established and, if this is after 1948, when planning controls commenced, the appropriate planning permissions should be produced. Similarly, if significant alterations have been made to the property in the last few years, any planning permission or building regulations consent should be requested.

- Perhaps the most common area of misunderstanding and dispute regarding replies to property information forms is which fixtures and fittings are going to be left and which are going to be removed. With increasing values attaching to all items of property, this question becomes increasingly significant and many firms have adopted the wise practice of preparing a lengthy schedule of all items which may be available and the seller is required to tick the appropriate column to indicate whether these are included or excluded. Check this list very carefully and report fully to the buyer. If there are areas of disagreement, these should be resolved at this stage. Under TransAction, there is a specific fixtures, fittings and contents form.

11.3 Bankruptcy search results

If the transaction is funded, then a lender will require a bankruptcy search against the name of the buyer before releasing the funds. The lender's conveyancer must submit a Form K16 to the Land Charges Department and, if there are any adverse entries, the lender must be told immediately.

11.4 Replies to requisitions on title

Sometimes, the seller's conveyancer may be unable to explain apparent defects in the title and, in such a case, the buyer's conveyancer is entitled to refuse to complete the transaction. Common defects in title have been referred to above.

If there are defects in title and the buyer nonetheless wishes to continue, such defects must be reported to the proposed mortgagee and its consent to proceeding must be obtained. Most common defects can be solved by obtaining a statutory declaration from those with knowledge of the property supported by a defective title indemnity policy. Such a measure would be regarded as one of last resort and, prior to that time, efforts may be made to rectify the title by contacting earlier owners. Such matters are carried out at the expense of the seller. Such problems generally do not apply to registered land.

It is important to obtain an undertaking to redeem all subsisting mortgages on completion. Frequently, the seller may well have a second mortgage registered against their title and, in these circumstances, it is most important to undertake a Form 94A Land Registry search in good time in order to see if any mortgages have been created recently.

11.5 Dealing with part of land comprised in a title

The starting point is the obtaining of a good plan which as accurately and precisely as possible defines the boundaries of the parcel of land to be conveyed. This plan should accord with a staked out area and, where possible, the boundary measurements should be included.

Form TP1 should be used to transfer the legal estate and must incorporate a plan and will commonly incorporate new restrictive covenants where the seller retains neighbouring property.

The Land Registry search is carried out on a Form 94B and, after completion of the purchase, the seller's certificate is put on deposit at the Land Registry for the purposes of having a part carved out of it.

The amended certificate is returned to the seller and a new certificate is issued to the buyer on completion of the registration.

12 The Rules of Professional Conduct

The practice of conveyancing is guided by rules of professional conduct, some of which relate uniquely to property transactions.

12.1 Rule 6 of the Solicitors' Practice Rules

A significant change for conveyancing practice was brought about by the new r 6 of the Solicitors' Practice Rules, which was introduced on 1 October 1999.

Rule 6 tightly regulates the conduct of a conveyance where the buyer is obtaining a mortgage and the mortgage lender has agreed to comply with r 6(3). This rule carefully defines the parameters of a solicitors responsibility when acting for the mortgage lender on a purchase and those cases governed by r 6(3) are characterised by the use of a standard certificate of title. The significance of this rule is that if it is not followed, then the practitioner is in breach of contract with the lender and in breach of professional conduct rules.

The aim of this section is to provide a brief synopsis of r 6 in order to indicate the basic parameters of the practitioner's responsibility. For a comprehensive statement of what is required by the rule, the reader is referred to the Rules of Professional Conduct:

- Rule 6 provides that if a practitioner or a member of his immediate family is a borrower, or if the practitioner proposes to act for a seller, buyer and lender in the same transaction, then the lender must be informed and they must then have an opportunity to decide whether to instruct, and if so whom.

- The certificate of title you give must be clear and therefore all enquiries and observations must be made before exchange of contracts.

- You must comply with the Law Society safeguards with regards to money laundering and fraud:

  (a) all deposits must be paid through solicitors and not between clients;

  (b) all allowances made for works, etc, must be pointed out whatever their size; and

  (c) you must verify the seller's conveyancers unless familiar with them.

- Identity – if the signatory to a document is not personally known to you, then you must get them to provide evidence of identity; any two of the following specified in the CML Handbook Part 2 will suffice – passport or photo ID and cheque guarantee card, Council Tax bill, rent book.

- Valuation – you must be supplied with a copy of the valuation. You must verify that the property description is correct and that the assumptions made regarding tenure and boundaries are correct and obviously that it has not been undervalued. You must not verify that its report contents are correct, as you are not a surveyor.

- You must notify the lender if the seller has not owned the property for at least six months unless it is an executor sale, repossession, developer, etc.

- Searches – you must carry out all reasonable searches – what are reasonable searches? Make sure you carry out a Commons Registration Act search whenever there is undeveloped land about, or a grass verge outside property. You should start thinking about environmental searches. If in doubt, get a search indemnity policy. Searches can only be three months old at exchange, and cannot be older than six months at completion. It might be cheaper to get indemnity insurance to extend the search rather than re-doing. Not all lenders accept personal searches – check!

- Planning – you should investigate that all planning conditions have been complied with. There must have been no unauthorised works done in the last four years, nor change of use in the last 10.

- Title – good leasehold title will only be acceptable if there is a marked abstract of the freehold 15 years before the grant of the lease, and that the title is good and marketable, and you get indemnity insurance. It is no longer good enough to say 'Well, it is old, therefore it is all right to accept anything less than absolute'. Title based on adverse possession title is satisfactory only if a statutory declaration for at least 12 years is produced, as well as indemnity insurance.

- Flying freehold – this will only be accepted if it is reported and a plan submitted, there are all the necessary rights of shelter and support, entry for repair and obligations for successors in title to carry these on; if these can't be satisfied, then indemnity insurance should be obtained. Check Part 2 of the certificate, as some lenders do not accept flying freeholds.

- Restrictive covenants – if there is a breach, then it must be investigated whether or not it is actually enforceable (that is, whether or not the 'benefit' has been capable of running with the land). A breach can be ignored if it is more than 20 years old, as no action is likely, and therefore lenders do not consider it will affect the security. If you cannot confirm that the breach is over 20 years old, then indemnity insurance must be obtained.

- Leaseholds – you should see Part 2 of the certificate for acceptable unexpired terms. Consent to an assignment should be obtained before completion. There should be all rights of support and access, and there must be adequate provisions for enforcement of covenants. Any increase in service charge for the coming year must be reported. You should make a company search against a management company. You must get your purchaser client to sign a blank stock transfer form to be placed with the deeds and place the Memorandum and Articles of Association with the deeds.

- Insolvency – you must obtain a clear bankruptcy search. If there are any entries, then you must get written confirmation that they do not apply.

- Deeds of gift – if you are aware that there has been a deed of gift in the last five years, or a transfer at an undervalue, then you must be satisfied that the lender is protected, so search against the donor and donee. If there is a risk, then indemnity insurance should be obtained.

- Price – you must confirm that the purchase price in the contract is the same as in the mortgage offer. You must report all cash back or allowance or non-cash incentive arrangements, whatever size, to the lender.

- Roads and sewers – the roads and sewers must be adopted, or a suitable bond agreement or bond should be in existence. If not, this must be reported.

- Easements – if the borrower owns adjoining land over which the borrower requires access to the property, or in respect of services, then this land must be mortgaged.

- Retentions – there is no obligation to release a retention, therefore do not give an undertaking to pay the retention to a third party.

- Grants – if the property is subject to a repair or improvement grant which is not being discharged or waived, then check Part 2 to see if it needs to be reported.

- Insurance – you must check that the borrower has suitable insurance in force up to the rebuilding cost in the valuation. Check Part 2 to see if details need to be reported. If the excess (£1,000) exceeds the amount in Part 2, then this must be reported.

- Occupiers – unless stated in Part 2, then all occupants aged 17 or over must sign a deed or form of consent.

- Indemnity insurance – a copy should be given to the borrower and a copy placed with the deeds.

- Certificate of title – the certificate of title should be unqualified.

- Funds – you are only authorised to release the loan when you hold sufficient funds to complete the purchase of the property, pay all stamp duty and registration fees. If you do not have these moneys then you must accept responsibility to pay these amounts yourself. You hold the loan on trust until completion.

- Delayed completion – you must notify the lender if completion does not take place as planned. See Part 2 for how long you should hold the funds.

- Registration – the application for registration must be received by the Land Registry during the priority period or for a first registration within two months of completion. You can now apply for an extension in writing. If you go past the time limit for first registration, then the legal estate reverts back to the seller and the Land Registry is under no obligation to register it.

- Deeds – these must be sent within the time limit set out in Part 2 or, at the latest, three months after completion. If this is not possible, then you must write to the lender to explain.

- Transfers of equity – you should check Part 2 for the specific requirements. Lenders only need to be a party to the transfer if they are being released. The covenant should be worded 'The new borrower agrees to pay the lender all the money due under the mortgage and will keep to all the terms of the mortgage'. If releasing the lender, then the clause should be: 'The lender releases [ ] from his/her obligations under the mortgage.' See Part 2 for the attestation clause.

12.2 Costs

Strictly, the solicitor incurs separate costs for acting on behalf of a lender and a scale of charges is suggested. In practice, most firms of solicitors do not now charge separately for dealing with the lender's formalities; it is included in the overall quotation provided. Of course, separate fees are applicable when acting only on a re-mortgage or a redemption. The new r 6 has given rise to debate about adding £200 to the standard fee.

12.3 Individual mortgage lenders

It is vital that the conveyancer should not act for both lender and borrower in a private mortgage situation. If you have two clients, or, for that matter, two members of the same family lending money to one another, one of those individuals must take separate and independent legal advice from another firm. However, although a loan between members of the same family may not be regarded as 'at arm's length' and, therefore, outside the scope of r 6, it is better to err on the side of caution.

12.4 Fraud

Sadly, over recent years, there has been a significant increase in the incidence of fraud. One of the most common instances in day to day private practice, where a solicitor can, possibly unwittingly, find himself involved in potential wrongdoing, is where a price for a property is renegotiated, and ends up being different from that notified to the mortgage lender. It is vital to make the mortgage lender aware of the correct purchase price, and that it is notified to the mortgage lender prior to completion of the mortgage.

In its warning to the profession about mortgage fraud, the Law Society has highlighted the following signs:

- A fictitious buyer – practitioners should beware of invented clients whom you never meet in person, and to whom you cannot speak on the telephone.
- Unusual instructions or an unusual transaction – if things go wrong in a transaction, there may be an innocent explanation, but equally, it may be that the behaviour of the clients, or those actually providing the instructions is irregular, because they have an unlawful design on the outcome.
- A deposit paid direct – if a deposit is paid direct from the buyer to the seller, you should ask why.

- Changes in the purchase price: this has been referred to above, and is probably the most common example of mortgage fraud. This happens particularly where a high percentage mortgage is required.

Certain steps can be taken to deal with the above situations:

- Insist on meeting the client.
- Question unusual instructions. Do not be afraid to challenge your instructions if they worry you.
- Discuss any odd cases or odd instructions with your partners or principal.
- Do not witness pre-signed documentation. Only witness documents that are signed in your presence. If documents are returned signed, but not witnessed, insist that they are re-signed in the presence of a witness.
- Check signatures: make sure that signatures on all documents are the same, to the extent that they purport to be by one and the same person.

There are a number of other examples of potential fraud which good and cautious conveyancing practice can eliminate. Full disclosure of a new mortgagee must be the order of the day.

Solicitors hardly need to be reminded that involvement, even passively or negligently, in a mortgage fraud is likely to constitute a criminal offence, and would, of course, lead to disciplinary proceedings.

12.5 Rule 6(2)

Rule 6(2) governs the ability of a solicitor to act for both seller and buyer, landlord and tenant and borrower and lender. In order to be able to act, a solicitor must satisfy two tests. First, if there is a conflict of interest, the solicitor cannot act. Secondly, if the first test is passed, the solicitor can only act for both parties if the transaction falls into one of the following categories:

- both parties are established clients;
- the consideration is £10,000 or less;
- there is no other qualified conveyancer in the area;
- the seller and buyer are represented by different offices of one firm and a different solicitor acts for each party. Remember, a solicitor cannot take advantage of this category if one office referred a party to another office.

12.6 Issuing a contract to more than one purchaser

The conduct of a contract race is a matter of concern and interest to the Law Society. Contract races are an example of a situation where a solicitor may be unwittingly involved in a difficult transaction, and therefore strict rules provided by the Law Society must be followed. The procedure applies regardless of whether the original contract is sent out simultaneously to both buyers' conveyancers or at different times.

Many conveyancers and estate agents go out of their way to avoid a contract race from the beginning. It is, of course, always open to a seller to withdraw a contract from a buyer and send out the contract to an alternative buyer's solicitor. In this way, only one contract is out at any given point in time, and the rules for the engagement of a contract race do not, therefore, come into play.

12.6.1 The rules

The buyer's conveyancer must be notified at once when a contract race is to begin. Notification must be made in writing. It is vital that the precise terms of the race are set out. Each buyer must know what has to be done in order to win the race. For example, it may well be that the seller agrees to exchange contracts with the first buyer to deposit a signed contract and deposit a cheque at the seller's conveyancer's office.

The clear terms of the contract race must be discussed with and explained to the seller. The seller might also be told that because there is so much anxiety involved in contract races, he could lose the interest of both prospective buyers. Great caution must be exercised.

The existence of a contract race is not affected by the decision of the seller to allow each contract to contain a different price.

12.7 Conflicts of interest

As explained above, conflict of interest rules must be carefully followed by conveyancers all the time. It is virtually impossible for the conveyancer to act for two prospective purchasers on a contract race and instructions must be declined in such a situation.

12.8 Undertakings in the conveyancing transaction

The provision of undertakings most commonly occurs on completion, where tasks remain to be fulfilled. It is particularly common with regard to the discharge of the seller's subsisting mortgage. Generally, such discharge cannot take place until the proceeds of sale become available to pay off that mortgage. Form DS1 (or discharge, under the ENDS system) will be sent to the buyer's conveyancer as soon as possible after completion and the appropriate form of undertaking, either in the Law Society's recommended form, or as part of the replies to the completion information and requisition on title form, will be given.

Another common occasion for the provision of an undertaking is when your client is to be responsible for someone else's costs. This may commonly occur when acting for the assignee of a lease or when a deed of easement is being granted. The extent of an undertaking as to costs in those cases should be limited by the provision of a maximum figure.

Undertakings must be carefully given with caution and on all occasions must be carefully worded. They are an obligatory commitment on the part of a solicitor and, for that matter, a licensed conveyancer. Breach of an undertaking can ultimately lead to disciplinary proceedings. It is professional misconduct. Once an undertaking has been fulfilled, a formal discharge should be requested.

In order to remind oneself that undertakings have been given on a particular file, the file should be carefully marked. This makes it apparent to anyone else dealing with that particular file that undertakings remain to be fulfilled. It is important not to do anything on that file which makes it impossible to fulfil the undertakings (for example, sending out the money to the client instead of using it to redeem a mortgage).

13 Tax

13.1 Value Added Tax

Generally, where land and buildings are concerned, the starting point is that any supply is VAT exempt. There are two main exceptions to this rule where VAT is chargeable. First, the freehold sale of new commercial buildings, where the liability to VAT extends from the date building works are commenced until either three years after practical completion or the first full year of occupation. Secondly, where the owner of a non-residential property 'opts to tax'. Following the election, the owner must charge VAT on any rents and the sale price of the property. On a purchase of commercial property, the intention to charge VAT is often referred to in the special conditions of the contract. A prospective tenant should also check the landlord's replies to preliminary enquiries to see whether VAT will be chargeable on the rent.

A tenanted building which would normally attract a charge of VAT (for the reasons set out above) on sale is relieved from VAT if the sale can be regarded as a 'transfer of a going concern'. Stringent conditions must be complied with if this relief is to be obtained.

Zero rating confers the ability to recover VAT on costs without having to charge VAT. The main situation when zero rating occurs is when a person has constructed a residential dwelling or has converted the whole or a part of a non-residential building into residential use and has, for the first time, granted either a registered lease or freehold interest in the property.

A solicitor whose professional costs are being paid by a third party (rather than his client) cannot render a VAT invoice to the third party. Nor should the third party be allowed to pay a solicitor's costs net of VAT. The third party must pay the professional costs plus VAT to the solicitor and seek to obtain a VAT invoice from the solicitor's client.

Remember that on a purchase of commercial property, stamp duty is chargeable on the VAT inclusive consideration.

13.2 Stamp duty

13.2.1 Exemptions from duty

Certain instruments are exempt from stamp duty totally and these are prescribed by the Stamp Duty (Exempt Instruments) Regulations 1987 SI 1987/516. In respect of purchases of houses at a discount from, for example, local authorities completed on or after 23 March 1981, duty is payable only on the actual discounted price paid. This is also the basis on which the land registration fee is payable. Section 110 of the Finance Act 1984 extended the list of bodies to which the Finance Act 1981 applies, so that it includes sales to a tenant by a housing association. Otherwise, all sales at a discount are liable to come to the attention of the appropriate district valuer who will then take it upon himself to inspect the property in order to decide on the actual valuation. It is on this valuation that stamp duty may subsequently be claimed by the Inland Revenue.

Instruments in favour of a charity, heritage or memorial fund are exempt from stamp duty, but must bear a stamp denoting this (s 129 of the Finance Act 1982).

Mortgage deeds do not attract stamp duty.

A transfer to a beneficiary under a will or the intestacy rules, divorce settlement transfers and lifetime gifts are the most common documents which are exempt from stamp duty. The exemption applies provided that the document contains a certificate specifying the category of exemption.

13.2.2 Transfers

Stamp duty is payable on the instrument of transfer within 30 days of completion.

Transfers of freehold property or leases for consideration of £500,000 or less will require a certificate of value. Where the purchase price of the property is £60,000 or less and the transaction does not form part of a larger transaction or series of transactions, no duty is payable provided that a certificate of value is included in the transfer. However, where the purchase price of property is greater than £60,000, then stamp duty is payable. At the time of writing, the rates of stamp duty are 1% (£60,001 to 250,000); 3% (£250,001 to £500,000) and 4% (over £500,000).

An exchange of freehold land for other freehold land attracts stamp duty at *ad valorem* rates. Duty is charged on each transfer on the open market value of each property.

Where a property is sold or a lease is granted for a price, premium or rent which is unascertainable, then stamp duty will be chargeable on the market value of the interest in land transferred.

13.2.3 Stamp duty and chattels

Stamp duty is not payable on chattels which are included in a sale. It is, therefore, permissible to apportion the purchase price between the chattels and the land. Stamp duty will only be chargeable on the value of the land. Apportionment in this way is particularly useful if the purchase price of the property is just above a stamp duty threshold. This apportionment must be agreed with the seller and reflected in the contract for sale. The apportionment must be realistic, and any overvaluation of chattels will be a fraud on the Inland Revenue.

13.2.4 Leases and agreements for leases

A lease which is presented for stamping must either contain a certificate to the effect that there was no prior agreement for lease or must be denoted with duty fully paid (if any).

The lease or agreement must be submitted to the Inland Revenue for the purpose of stamping in the same way as a transfer deed. The same time limit applies. The amount of duty payable depends on the rent and the term of the lease.

Added to the rent is VAT, whether this is actually payable or not. The stamp duty is payable on the gross figure of the rent plus VAT at the current rate. It is important to remember that the counterpart lease should be stamped with a fixed duty of £5.

Where the rent is variable, the average annual rent for the term from the date of execution is taken.

A lease granted for a fixed term and thereafter until determined is treated as for a definite term equal to the fixed term together with such further period as must elapse before the earliest date at which the lease can be determined.

Stamp duty on leases is payable according to the length of the term. The scale is as follows:

- not more than seven years – 1%;
- more than seven years but not more than 35 years – 2%;
- more than 35 years but not more than 100 years – 12%;
- over 100 years – 24%.

With regard to premiums, the stamp duty chargeable on the premium is as follows:

- if the premium is not more than £60,000 and the annual rent is not more than £600 – nil duty;
- if the annual rent exceeds £600 – 1%;
- over £60,000 premium but not more than £250,000 – 1%;
- over £250,000 but not more than £500,000 – 3%;
- premiums over £500,000 – 4%.

An alternative to calculating the stamp duty payable on a lease is to ask the stamp duty to be 'marked' by the Stamp Office. When the Stamp Office 'mark' a lease, they calculate the appropriate level of duty payable.

13.2.5 Further information

If you have any queries regarding stamp duty, then we recommend that you contact the Stamp Office by telephone on 0845 603 0135 or look at their website at www.inlandrevenue.gov.uk/so.

13.3 Capital Gains Tax

The incidence of CGT is a very important consideration when a client is proposing a deed of gift or when a client is purchasing a property in which he does not intend to live.

The disposal of an individual's principal private dwelling house is exempt from CGT. A degree of permanence at the dwelling house is required for the exemption to be claimed.

However, the following are associated exceptions to the above rule:

- relief may be lost if the garden annexed to the dwelling house is greater than 0.5 hectares;
- no relief is available on the sale of a garden when it is sold separately from the house and after the sale of the house;

- where part of the property is used for commercial purposes, then part of the exemption will be lost;
- no relief is available for a holiday home;
- where a married couple own more than one dwelling house, then an election must be made as to which property has the benefit of the exemption. Such an election is not irrevocable;
- no relief is available if a person buys his dwelling house in the name of a company;
- it is easy to overlook the possibility of payment of CGT when dealing with a gift, or indeed if the property forms part of an inheritance which is then not lived in and subsequently sold then, subject to the allowances, CGT will be payable upon any gain made.

13.3.1 Payment of CGT

It is important to remember that each spouse has an annual allowance for CGT purposes. It may be that any increase in the value of a property will fall within this annual exemption. However, any other gains made in the tax year will also be taken into account, in order to provide an aggregate gain for the purposes of the clients CGT liability.

Companies pay CGT at the corporation tax rate applicable subject to roll-over relief.

A disposal of a property is made at the time of the contract and not at the time of completion. It is the date of the contract that is used for the purposes of assessment to tax, although clearly no tax becomes payable until the contract is completed.

14 Forms and Precedents

Form Con 29

CON 29 (2000) SUBSTITUTE
To be submitted in duplicate

ENQUIRIES OF LOCAL AUTHORITY (2000) EDITION

A. To

B. Property

C. Other roadways, footpaths and footways

D.

E.

F. Reply to

A Enter name and address of District or Borough Council for the area. If the property is near a local authority boundary, consider raising certain enquiries (e.g. Road schemes) with the adjoining Council.

B Enter address and description of the property. A plan in duplicate must be attached if possible and is insisted upon by some Councils. Without a plan, replies may be inaccurate or incomplete. A plan is essential for optional enquiries 18, 37 and 38.

C Enter name and / or location of (and mark on plan if possible) any other roadways, footpaths and footways (in addition to those entered in box B) for enquiry 3 and (if raised) enquiries 19 and 20.

D Answer every question. Any additional enquiries must be attached on a seperate sheet in duplicate and an additional fee will be charged for any that the Council is willing to answer.

E Details of fees can be obtained from the Council or The Law Society.

F Enter name and address of the person or firm lodging this form

G Tick which optional enquiries are to be answered

G	Optional Enquiries
17.	Road proposals by private bodies
18.	Public path and byways
19.	Permanent road closure
20.	Traffic schemes
21.	Advertisements
22.	Completion notices
23.	Parks and countryside
24.	Pipe lines
25.	Houses in multiple occupation
26.	Noise abatement
27.	Urban development areas
28.	Enterprise zones
29.	Inner urban improvement areas
30.	Simplified planning zones
31.	Land maintenance notices
32.	Mineral consultation areas
33.	Hazardous substance consents
34.	Environmental and pollution notices
35.	Food safety notices
36.	Radon gas precautions
37.	Sewers within the property
38.	Nearby sewers

PART 1 - STANDARD ENQUIRIES
(APPLICABLE IN EVERY CASE)
DEVELOPMENT PLANS AND PROVISIONS

Structure Plan

1.1.1   What structure plan is in force ?

1.1.2   Have any proposals been made public for the alteration of the structure plan ?
Local Plans

1.2.1   What stage has been reached in preparation of a local plan?

1.2.2   Have any proposals been made public for the alteration or replacement of a local plan ?
Old Style Development Plan

1.3   What old style development plan is in force ?

Unitary Development Plan

1.4.1   What stage has been reached in the preparation of an unitary development plan ?

1.4.2   Have any proposals been made public for the alteration or replacement of a unitary development plan ?
Non Statutory Plan

1.5.1   Have the Council made public any proposals for the preparation or modification of a non-statutory plan ?

1.5.2   If so, what stage has been reached?

Policies or Proposals for the Property

1.6   Do any of the above plans (including any proposed alterations or replacements) indicate:-
(a) a designation of primary use or zoning for the property or the area, or

(b) a specific proposal which includes the property ?

Land required for public purposes

1.7   Is the property included in any of the categories of land specified in Schedule 13 Paras 5 and 6 of The T& CP Act 1990 ?
DRAINAGE
Foul Drainage

2.1.1   To the Councils Knowledge, does foul drainage from the property drain to a public sewer ?

2.1.2   If yes, does the property drain into a public sewer through
(a) a private drain alone, or
(b) a private drain and then a private sewer ? (3,4,5)

Surface Water Drainage

2.2.1   To the Councils Knowledge, does surface water from the property drain to-
(a) a public sewer,or
(b) a highway drain (3,4,5)

2.2.2   If the answer to 2.2.1. (a) or (b) is yes, does the surface water drain to it through:
(a) a private drain alone, or
(b) a private drain and then a private sewer ? (3,4,5)

Statutory Agreements and Consents

2.3.1   Is there in force an agreement under s.22 of the Building Act 1984 for drainage of any part of the property in combination with another building through a private sewer ?

2.3.2 Except as shown in the Official Certificate of Search, is there in force an agreement or consent under s.18 of The Building Act 1984 for the erection of a building or extension of a building over or in the vicinity of a drain, sewer or disposal main ? (4)

Adoption Agreement

2.4.1 To the Council's knowledge, is any sewer serving, or which is proposed to serve, the property the subject of an agreement under s.104 of The Water Industry Act 1991 for the sewer to become vested in the sewerage undertaker ? (5,6)

2.4.2 If so, is such an agreement supported by a bond or other financial security ? (6)

Sewerage Undertaker

2.5 Please state the name and address of the sewerage undertaker?

MAINTENANCE OF ROADS etc

Publicly Maintained

3.1 Are all the roadways, footpaths and footways referred to in Boxes B and C on page 1 maintainable at the public expense within the meaning of the Highways Act 1980 ? (7)

Resolutions to Make Up or Adopt

3.2 If not, have the Council passed any resolution to:-
(a) make up any of those roadways, footpaths or footways at the cost of the frontagers, or
(b) adopt any of them without cost to the frontagers ?
If so, please specify (7)

Adoption Agreements

3.3.1 Have the Council entered into any subsisting agreement relating to the adoption of any of those roadways, footpaths or footways ? If so, please specify? (6)

3.3.2 Is any such agreement supported by a bond or other financial security ? (6)

ROAD SCHEMES

Trunk and Special Roads

4.1.1 What orders, draft orders or schemes have been notified to the Council by the appropriate Secretary of State for the construction of a new trunk or special road, the centre line of which is within 200 metres of the property ?

4.1.2 What proposals have been notified to the Council by the Secretary of State for -
(a) the alteration or improvement of an existing road, involving the construction, whether or not within existing highway limits, of a subway, underpass, flyover, footbridge, elevated road or dual carriageway, the centre line of which is within 200 metres of the property, or
(b) the construction of a roundabout (other than a mini roundabout (8), or the widening of an existing road by the construction of more additional traffic lanes, the limits of construction of which are within 200 metres of the property?

Other Roads

4.2 What proposals of their own (9) have the Council approved for any of the following, the limits of construction of which are within 200 metres of the property :-
(a) the construction of a new road, or

(b) the alteration or improvement of an existing road, involving the construction, whether or not within existing highway limits, of a subway, underpass, flyover, footbridge, elevated road, dual carriageway, the construction of a roundabout (other than a mini roundabout (8)), or the widening of an existing road by the construction of one or more additional traffic lanes ?

Road Proposals Involving Acquisition

4.3   What proposals have the Council approved, or have been
       notified to the Council by the appropriate Secretary of State, for
       highway construction or improvement that involve the acquisition
       of the property ?

Road Proposals at Consultation Stage

4.4   What proposals have either the Secretary of State or the Council
       published for public consultation relating to :- -.
       (a) the construction of a new road indicating a possible route the
       centre line of which would be likely to be within 200 metres of the
       property, or
       (b) the alteration or improvement of an existing road, involving
       the construction, whether or not within existing highways limits, of
       a subway, underpass, flyover, footbridge, elevated road, dual
       carriageway, the construction of a roundabout (other than a mini
       roundabout (8), or the widening of an existing road by the
       construction of one or more additional traffic lanes, the limits of
       the construction of which would likely to be within 200 metres of
       the property ?

       Answers to road schemes are obtained from Highways direct or
       information contained within their "Local Transport Plan"

OUTSTANDING NOTICES

5   What outstanding statutory notices have been issued by the
       Council under The Public Health Acts, Housing Acts, Highways
       Acts, Building Acts (10) or Part III or the Enviromental Protection
       Act 1990 ?

BUILDING REGULATIONS

6   What proceedings have the Council authorised in respect of an
       infringement of The Building Regulations ?

PLANNING APPLICATIONS AND PERMISSIONS

Applications and Decisions

7.1   Please list:-
       (a) any entries in the Register of planning applications and
       permissions.
       (b) any applications and decisions in respect of Listed building
       consent.
       (c) any applications and decisions in respect of conservation area
       consent.

Inspection and Copies

7.2   If there are any entries:
       (a) how can copies of the decisions be obtained ?
       (b) where can that Register be inspected ?

NOTICES UNDER PLANNING ACTS

Enforcement and Stop Notices

8.1.1   Please list any entries in the Register of enforcement notices and
        stop notices.

8.1.2   If there are any entries:
        (a) how can copies of the notices be obtained ?
        (b) where can that Register be inspected ?

Enforcement Notices or Stop Notices

8.2   Except as shown in the Official Certificate of Search, or in reply
        to enquiry 8.1.1 has any enforcement notice, listed building
        enforcement notice, or stop notice been authorised by the
        Council for issue or service (other than notices which have been
        withdrawn or quashed) ?

Compliance with Enforcement Notices

8.3   If an enforcement notice or listed building enforcement notice has
        been served or issued, has it been complied with to the
        satisfaction of the Council ?

Other Planning Notices

8.4 Have the Council served, or resolved to serve, any breach of condition or planning contravention notice or any other notice or proceedings relating to a breach of planning control ?

Listed Building Repair Notices etc

8.5.1 To the knowledge of the Council, has the service or a repairs notice been authorised ?

8.5.2 If the Council have authorised the making of an order for the compulsory acquisition of a listed building is a "minimum compensation" provision included, or to be included in the order ?

8.5.3 Have the Council authorised the service of a building preservation notice ? (11)

DIRECTIONS RESTRICTING PERMITTED DEVELOPMENT

9 Except as shown in the Official Certificate of Search, have the Council made a direction to restrict permitted development ?

ORDERS UNDER PLANNING ACTS

Revocation Orders etc

10.1 Except as shown in the Official Certificate of Search, have the Council made any Orders revoking or modifying any planning permission or discontinuing an existing planning use ?

Tree Preservation Order

10.2 Except as shown in the Official Certificate of Search, have the Council made any Tree Preservation Orders ?

COMPENSATION FOR PLANNING DECISIONS

11 What compensation has been paid by the Council under s.114 of the T&CP Act 1990 for planning decisions restricting development other than new development?

CONSERVATION AREA

12 Except as shown in the Official Certificate of Search, is the area a conservation area?

COMPULSORY PURCHASE ORDER

13 Except as shown in the Official Certificate of Search, have the Council made any order (whether or not confirmed by the appropriate Secretary of State) or passed any resolution for compulsory acquisition which is still capable of being implemented (12) ?

AREAS DESIGNATED UNDER HOUSING ACTS etc

Clearance

14.1 Has any programme of clearance for the area been :-
(a) Submitted to the Department of the Environment or

(b) Resolved to be submitted or
(c) Otherwise adopted by resolution of the Council ?

Housing

14.2 Except as shown in the Official Certificate of Search, have the Council resolved to define the area as designated for a purpose under the Housing Acts ? If so, please specify the purpose.

SMOKE CONTROL ORDER

15 Except as shown in the Official Certificate of Search, have the Council made a Smoke Control Order or resolved to make or vary a Smoke Control Order for the area ?

RAILWAYS

16   What proposals have been notified to the Council, and what
        proposals of their own have the Council approved, for the
        construction of a railway (including light railway or monorail) the
        centre line of which is within 200 metres of the property ?

CONTAMINATED LAND

Register Entries

16.A.1 Please list any entries maintained under s.78R(1) of the
        enviromental Protection Act 1990 in relation to the property

        Notice of Identification of Contaminated Land

16.A.2 Has the Council served any notice under s.78 Pt (3) in relation to
        the property ?

        Consultation as to Adjoining or Adjacent Contaminated Land

16.A.3 Has the Council consulted with the owner or occupier of the
        property under s.78G(3) in relation to anything to be done on the
        property as a result of adjoining or adjacent land being
        contaminated land ?

        Identification of Risk from Adjoining or Adjacent Land

16.A.4 Has any entry been made in the register, or has any notice been
        served in relation to any adjoining or adjacent land which has
        been identified as contaminated land because it is in such a
        condition that harm or pollution of controlled waters might be
        caused on the property ?

        Negative answers do not imply that the property or any adjoining
        or adjacent land is free from contamination or from the risk of it.
        Enquiries 16A.3 and 16A.4 may not disclose steps taken by
        another Council in whose area or adjoining or adjacent land is
        situated

PART II

18   Is any public path, bridleway or road used as a public path or
        byway, which abuts on (7) or crosses the property shown in a
        definitive map or revised definitive map prepared under part IV
        of the National Parks and Access to the Countryside Act 1949,
        or, part III of the Wildlife and Countryside Act 1981 ?. If so,
        please mark it's approximate route on the attached plan (14).

Form LLC1

Form LLC1. (*Local Land Charges Rules 1977 Schedule 1, Form C*)

**The duplicate of this form must also be completed:
a carbon copy will suffice**

For directions, notes and fees see overleaf

Insert name and address of registering authority in space below

Suffolk Coastal District Council
Council Offices
Melton Hill
WOODBRIDGE
Suffolk
IP12 1AU

Official Number
(*To be completed by the registering authority*)

Register of local land charges

Requisition for search

and official certificate

of search

Requisition for search
(*A separate requisition must be made in respect of each parcel of
land except as explained overleaf*)

An official search is required in ~~PART~~ the whole _of_[1]
the register of local land charges kept by the above-named
registering authority for subsisting registrations against the land
[defined in the attached plan and][2] described below.

Description of land sufficient to enable it to be identified

Hatherleigh Farmhouse Saxmundham Road Framlingham Woodbridge Suffolk

Name and address to which certificate is to be sent

Ross Coates
139 Main Road
Kesgrave
IPSWICH
Suffolk
IP5 7NP

Signature of applicant (*or his solicitor*)

Ross Coates

Date
12th July 1996

Telephone number
(01473) 621800

Reference
RMC/C/CLAYTON

Enclosure
Cheque ~~Money Order Postal Order value £~~

Official certificate of search

*To be completed by
authorised officer*

It is hereby certified that the search requested above reveals
no subsisting registrations[3]

or the_____registrations described in the Schedule
hereto[3] up to and including the date of this certificate.

Signed ....

On behalf of ....[4]

Date

1 Delete if inappropriate. Otherwise insert Part(s) in which
search is required.

2 Delete if inappropriate. (A plan should be furnished
in duplicate if it is desired that a copy should be returned.)

3 Delete inapplicable words. (The Parts of the Schedule should
be securely attached to the certificate and the number of
registrations disclosed should be inserted in the space provided.
Only Parts which disclose subsisting registrations should be sent.)

4 Insert name of registering authority.

Form 96

Application for an **Official Search** of the Index Map (Note 1)	HM Land Registry	Form **96**

FOR EXPLANATORY NOTES SEE OVERLEAF
Please complete in typescript or in BLACK BLOCK LETTERS all details within the thick black lines.

(Rule 9 Land Registration (Open Register) Rules 1991)

To The Kingston Upon Hull District Land Registry

DX 26700
HULL 4

(Note 2)

For official use only	
Description	Date
Fees Debited £	Record of Fees paid

I   ROSS COATES

of   139 Main Road   Kesgrave   Ipswich
Suffolk

(enter name and address of person or firm making the application)

apply for an official search of the Index Map or General Map and Parcels Index, and the list of pending applications for first registration, in respect of the land referred to below and shown | edged red | on the attached plan.

NOTE - Any attached plan must contain sufficient details of the surrounding roads and other features to enable the land to be identified satisfactorily on the Ordnance Survey Map. However, a plan may be unnecessary if the land can be identified by postal description. Nevertheless, the Chief Land Registrar reserves the right to ask for a plan to be supplied where he considers it necessary.

PAYMENT OF FEE (Note 4)

Please enter X in the appropriate box:–

☐ the Land Registry fee of £ ____ accompanies this application,

or

☒ please debit the Credit Account mentioned below with the appropriate fee payable under the current Land Registration Fees Order.

FOR COMPLETION BY APPLICANTS WHO ARE CREDIT ACCOUNT HOLDERS

YOUR KEY NUMBER:-

1	2	3	4	5	6

YOUR REFERENCE:-

R	M	C		C	L	A	

Signed *Ross Coates*

Date   12th July 1996

Telephone No.   (01473) 621800

Reference   RMC/C/CLA

HM Land Registry

Property   Hatherleigh Farmhouse
Postal number or description

Name of road   Saxmundham Road

Name of locality   Framlingham

Town   Woodbridge

Postcode   IP13 9PH

District or London Borough   Suffolk : Suffolk Coastal

Administrative County   Suffolk

Ordnance Survey Map Reference   (Note 3)

Known Title Number(s)

Enter Name and either address including postcode OR (if applicable) DX number of the person to whom the official certificate of result of search is to be sent.

Ross Coates
Solicitor
139 Main Road
Kesgrave
IPSWICH
Suffolk
IP5 7NP

Reference   RMC/C/CLAYTON

CERTIFICATE OF RESULT OF OFFICIAL SEARCH OF THE INDEX MAP   (Form 96 Result)

It is certified that the official search applied for has been made with the following result :- (Only the statements opposite the boxes marked X apply.)

☐ The land _____ is not registered. (Note 5)

☐ The land _____ is not affected by any caution against first registration or any priority notice.

☐ The land _____ is affected by a pending application for first registration under the following reference

☐ The land _____ is registered freehold under Title No.

☐ The land _____ is registered leasehold under Title No.

☐ The land _____ is affected by a rentcharge under Title No.

☐ The land _____ is affected by a caution against first registration/ priority notice under Title No.

Official stamp

When applying for first registration of the above property or writing in relation to it, please enclose this result of search and any plan annexed thereto.

Contract of sale

AGREEMENT
(Incorporating the Standard Conditions of Sale (Third Edition))

Agreement date	:	1996
Seller	:	RODNEY STEVEN CLAYTON and PATRICIA MARIA CLAYTON both of Hatherleigh Farmhouse Saxmundham Road Framlingham Woodbridge Suffolk
Buyer	:	BRIAN CLIFFORD GARRATT of The School Parham Woodbridge Suffolk
Property (freehold/~~leasehold~~)	:	Freehold property situate at and known as Hatherleigh Farmhouse Saxmundham Road Framlingham in the County of Suffolk as the same is for the purpose of identification only shown edged red on the plan attached hereto.
~~Root of title~~/**Title Number**	:	SK12345
Incumbrances on the Property	:	As disclosed by the Charges Register of the said title number.
Title Guarantee (full/~~limited~~)	:	
Completion date	:	1996
Contract rate	:	4% above Lloyds Bank Plc base lending rate from time to time in force
Purchase price	:	£250,000.00
Deposit	:	£ 25,000.00
Amount payable for chattels	:	
Balance	:	£225,000.00

The Seller will sell and the Buyer will buy the Property for the Purchase price.
The Agreement continues on the back page.

WARNING	Signed
This is a formal document, designed to create legal rights and legal obligations. Take advice before using it.	Seller/Buyer

SPECIAL CONDITIONS

1. (a) This Agreement incorporates the Standard Conditions of Sale (Third Edition). Where there is a conflict between those Conditions and this Agreement, this Agreement prevails.

   (b) Terms used or defined in this Agreement have the same meaning when used in the Conditions.

2. The Property is sold subject to the Incumbrances on the Property and the Buyer will raise no requisitions on them.

3. Subject to the terms of this Agreement and to the Standard Conditions of Sale, the seller is to transfer the property with the title guarantee specified on the front page.

4. The chattels on the Property and set out on any attached list are included in the sale.

5. The Property is sold with vacant possession on completion.

(or) 5. The Property is sold subject to the following leases or tenancies:

6. The Purchasers proceed on the basis of their own survey and inspection and hereby acknowledge that they do not rely on any representations by or on behalf of the Seller save those given in written replies to enquiries by the Sellers Solicitors.

Seller's Solicitors : Ross Coates Solicitor 139 Main Road Kesgrave Ipswich Suffolk IP5 7NP

Buyer's Solicitors : Messrs Ling & Co. 5 Bridge Street Framlingham Woodbridge Suffolk IP13 9DR

©1995 **OYEZ** The Solicitors' Law Stationery Society Ltd, Oyez House, 7 Spa Road, London SE16 3QQ

4.95 F29334
5065046
★ ★
3rd Edition

© 1995 **THE LAW SOCIETY**

Standard Conditions of Sale

CONTRACT
(Incorporating the Standard Commercial Property Conditions (First Edition))

Contract date :

Seller :

Buyer :

Property :
(freehold/leasehold)

Root of title/Title Number :

Incumbrances on the Property :

Completion date :

Contract rate :

Purchase price :

Deposit :

Amount payable for chattels :

The Seller will sell and the Buyer will buy the Property for the Purchase price.
The Contract continues on the back page

WARNING	Signed
This is a formal document, designed to create legal rights and legal obligations. Take advice before using it.	Authorised to sign on behalf of Seller/Buyer

STANDARD COMMERCIAL PROPERTY CONDITIONS (FIRST EDITION)

GENERAL

Definitions:

1 In these conditions:

(a) "accrued interest" means:
  (i) if money has been placed on deposit or in a building society share account, the interest actually earned
  (ii) otherwise, the interest which might reasonably have been earned by depositing the money at interest on seven days' notice of withdrawal with a clearing bank
  less, in either case, any proper charges for handling the money

(b) "clearing bank" means a member of CHAPS Clearing Limited

(c) "completion date", unless otherwise defined, has the meaning given in condition 6.1.1

(d) "contract rate", unless otherwise defined is the Law Society's interest rate from time to time in force

(e) "direct credit" means a direct transfer of cleared funds to an account nominated by the seller's solicitor and held at a clearing bank

(f) "lease" includes sub-lease, tenancy and agreement for a lease or sub-lease

(g) "notice to complete" means a notice requiring completion of the contract in accordance with condition 6

(h) "public requirement" means any notice, order or proposal given or made (whether before or after the date of the contract) by a body acting on statutory authority

(i) "requisition" includes objection

(j) "service charge" has the meaning given to it by section 18 of the Landlord and Tenant Act 1985 (disregarding the words "of a dwelling")

(k) "solicitor" includes barrister, certificated notary public, licensed conveyancer and recognised body under sections 9 or 32 of the Administration of Justice Act 1985

(l) "transfer" includes conveyance and assignment

(m) "working day" means any day from Monday to Friday (inclusive) which is not Christmas Day, Good Friday or a statutory Bank Holiday.

2 When used in these conditions the terms "absolute title" and "office copies" have the special meanings given to them by the Land Registration Act 1925.

Joint parties

If there is more than one seller or more than one buyer, the obligations which they undertake can be enforced against them all jointly or against each individually.

Notices and documents

1 A notice required or authorised by the contract must be in writing.

2 Giving a notice or delivering a document to a party's solicitor has the same effect as giving or delivering it to that party.

3 Transmission by fax is a valid means of giving a notice or delivering a document where delivery of the original document is not essential.

4 Subject to conditions 1.3.5 to 1.3.7, a notice is given and a document delivered when it is received.

5 If a notice or document is received after 4.00 p.m. on a working day, or on a day which is not a working day, it is to be treated as having been received on the next working day.

6 Unless the actual time of receipt is proved, a notice or document sent by the following means is to be treated as having been received before 4.00p.m. on the day shown below:

(a) by first class post:	two working days after posting
(b) by second-class post:	three working days after posting
(c) through a document exchange:	on the first working day after the day on which it would normally be available for collection by the addressee.

.7 Where a notice or document is sent through a document exchange, then for the purposes of condition 1.3.6 the actual time of receipt is:

(a) the time when the addressee collects it from the document exchange or, if earlier

(b) 8.00 a.m. on the first working day on which it is available for collection at that time.

VAT

1 An obligation to pay money includes an obligation to pay any value added tax chargeable in respect of that payment.

2 All sums made payable by the contract are exclusive of value added tax.

Assignment and Sub-sales

1 The buyer is not entitled to transfer the benefit of the contract.

2 The seller may not be required to transfer the property in parts or to any person other than the buyer.

FORMATION

Date

1 If the parties intend to make a contract by exchanging duplicate copies by post or through a document exchange, the contract is made when the last copy is posted or deposited at the document exchange.

2 If the parties' solicitors agree to treat exchange as taking place before duplicate copies are actually exchanged, the contract is made as so agreed.

Deposit

1 The buyer is to pay a deposit of 10 per cent of the purchase price no later than the date of the contract.

2 Except on a sale by auction the deposit is to be paid by direct credit and is to be held by the seller's solicitor as stakeholder on terms that on completion it is paid to the seller with accrued interest.

Auctions

1 On a sale by auction the following conditions apply to the property and, if it is sold in lots, to each lot.

2 The sale is subject to a reserve price.

3 The seller, or a person on its behalf, may bid up to the reserve price.

4 The auctioneer may refuse any bid.

5 If there is a dispute about a bid, the auctioneer may resolve the dispute or restart the auction at the last undisputed bid.

6 The auctioneer is to hold the deposit as agent for the seller. If any cheque tendered in payment of all or part of the deposit is dishonoured when first presented, the seller may, within seven working days of being notified that the cheque has been dishonoured, give notice to the buyer that the contract is discharged by the buyer's breach.

MATTERS AFFECTING THE PROPERTY

Freedom from incumbrances

1 The seller is selling the property free from incumbrances, other than those mentioned in condition 3.1.2.

2 The incumbrances subject to which the property is sold are:

(a) those mentioned in the contract

(b) those discoverable by inspection of the property before the contract

(c) those the seller does not and could not reasonably know about

(d) matters, other than monetary charges or incumbrances, disclosed or which would have been disclosed by the searches and enquiries which a prudent buyer would have made before entering into the contract

(e) public requirements.

3 After the contract is made, the seller is to give the buyer written details without delay of any new public requirement and of anything in writing which it learns about concerning any incumbrances subject to which the property is sold.

4 The buyer is to bear the cost of complying with any outstanding public requirement and is to indemnify the seller against any liability resulting from a public requirement.

Physical state

1 The buyer accepts the property in the physical state it is in at the date of the contract unless the seller is building or converting it.

2 A leasehold property is sold subject to any subsisting breach of a condition or tenant's obligation relating to the physical state of the property which renders the lease liable to forfeiture.

3 A sub-lease is granted subject to any subsisting breach of a condition or tenant's obligation relating to the physical state of the property which renders the seller's own lease liable to forfeiture.

Leases affecting the property

.1 The following provisions apply if any part of the property is sold subject to a lease.

.2 The seller having provided the buyer with full details of each lease or copies of the documents embodying the lease terms, the buyer is treated as entering into the contract knowing and fully accepting those terms.

.3 (a) The seller is to inform the buyer without delay if the seller learns of any application by the tenant in connection with the lease.

(b) The seller is not to agree to any application by the tenant nor to grant or withhold licences, consents or approvals required under the lease without the consent of the buyer.

(c) The buyer is not to withhold its consent or attach conditions to the consent where to do so might place the seller in breach of an obligation to the tenant or a statutory duty.

(d) In all other circumstances the seller is to act as the buyer reasonably directs, and the buyer is to indemnify it against all consequent loss and expense.

3.3.4 The seller is not to agree to any proposal to change the lease terms without the consent of the buyer and is to inform the buyer without delay of any change which may be proposed or agreed.

3.3.5 The seller is to manage the property in accordance with the principles of good estate management until completion.

3.3.6 The seller is to inform the buyer without delay if the lease ends and is not to serve any notice to end the lease.

3.3.7 The buyer is to indemnify the seller against all claims arising from the lease after actual completion; this includes claims which are unenforceable against a buyer for want of registration.

3.3.8 If the property does not include all the land let, the seller may apportion the rent and, if the lease is a new tenancy, the buyer may require the seller to apply under section 10 of the Landlord and Tenant (Covenants) Act 1995 for the apportionment to bind the tenant.

3.4 **Retained land**

3.4.1 The following provisions apply where after the transfer the seller will be retaining land near the property.

3.4.2 The buyer will have no right of light or air over the retained land, but otherwise the seller and the buyer will each have the rights over the land of the other which they would have had if they were two separate buyers to whom the seller had made simultaneous transfers of the property and the retained land.

3.4.3 Either party may require that the transfer is to contain appropriate express terms.

4. **TITLE AND TRANSFER**

4.1 **Timetable**

4.1.1 The following are the steps for deducing and investigating the title to the property to be taken within the following time limits:

Step	Time Limit
1. The seller is to send the buyer evidence of title in accordance with condition 4.2	Immediately after making the contract
2. The buyer may raise written requisitions	Six working days after either the date of the contract or the date of delivery of the seller's evidence of title on which the requisitions are raised whichever is the later
3. The seller is to reply in writing to any requisitions raised	Four working days after receiving the requisitions
4. The buyer may make written observations on the seller's replies	Three working days after receiving the replies

The time limit on the buyer's right to raise requisitions applies even where the seller supplies incomplete evidence of its title, but the buyer may, within six working days from delivery of any further evidence, raise further requisitions resulting from that evidence. On the expiry of the relevant time limit the buyer loses its right to raise requisitions or make observations.

4.1.2 The parties are to take the following steps to prepare and agree the transfer of the property within the following time limits:

Step	Time Limit
A. The buyer is to send the seller a draft transfer	At least twelve working days before completion date
B. The seller is to approve or revise that draft and either return it or retain it for use as the actual transfer	Four working days after delivery of the draft transfer
C. If the draft is returned the buyer is to send an engrossment to the seller	At least five working days before completion date

4.1.3 Periods of time under conditions 4.1.1 and 4.1.2 may run concurrently.

4.1.4 If the period between the date of the contract and completion date is less than 15 working days, the time limits in conditions 4.1.1 and 4.1.2 are to be reduced by the same proportion as that period bears to the period of 15 working days. Fractions of a working day are to be rounded down except that the time limit to perform any step is not to be less than one working day.

4.2 **Proof of title**

4.2.1 The evidence of registered title is office copies of the items required to be furnished by section 110(1) of the Land Registration Act 1925 and the copies, abstracts and evidence referred to in section 110(2).

4.2.2 The evidence of unregistered title is an abstract of the title, or an epitome of title with photocopies of the relevant documents.

4.2.3 Where the title to the property is unregistered, the seller is to produce to the buyer (without cost to the buyer):

(a) the original of every relevant document, or

(b) an abstract, epitome or copy with an original marking by a solicitor of examination against the original or against an examined abstract or against an examined copy.

4.3 **Defining the property**

4.3.1 The seller need not:

(a) prove the exact boundaries of the property

(b) prove who owns fences, ditches, hedges or walls

(c) separately identify parts of the property with different titles

further than it may be able to do from information in its possession.

4.3.2 The buyer may, if to do so is reasonable, require the seller to make or obtain, pay for and hand over a statutory declaration about facts relevant to the matters mentioned in condition 4.3.1. The form of the declaration is to be agreed by the buyer, who must not unreasonably withhold its agreement.

4.4 **Rents and rentcharges**

The fact that a rent or rentcharge, whether payable or receivable by the owner of the property, has been or will on completion be, informally apportioned is not to be regarded as a defect in title.

4.5 **Transfer**

4.5.1 The buyer does not prejudice its right to raise requisitions, or to require replies to any raised, by taking any steps in relation to the preparation or agreement of the transfer.

4.5.2 If the contract makes no provision as to title guarantee, then subject to condition 4.5.4 the seller is to transfer the property with full title guarantee.

4.5.3 The transfer is to have effect as if the disposition is expressly made subject to all matters to which the property is sold subject under the terms of the contract.

4.5.4 If after completion the seller will remain bound by any obligation affecting the property and disclosed to the buyer before the contract is made, but the law does not imply any covenant by the buyer to indemnify the seller against liability for future breaches of it:

(a) the buyer is to covenant in the transfer to indemnify the seller against liability for any future breach of the obligation and to perform it from then on, and

(b) if required by the seller, the buyer is to execute and deliver to the seller on completion a duplicate transfer prepared by the buyer.

4.5.5 The seller is to arrange at its expense that, in relation to every document of title which the buyer does not receive on completion, the buyer is to have the benefit of:

(a) a written acknowledgement of the buyer's right to its production, and

(b) a written undertaking for its safe custody (except while it is held by a mortgagee or by someone in a fiduciary capacity).

5 **PENDING COMPLETION**

5.1 **Responsibility for property**

5.1.1 Unless condition 5.1.2 or condition 8.1.3 applies:

(a) the seller is under no obligation to the buyer to insure the property

(b) if payment under a policy effected by or for the buyer is reduced, because the property is covered against loss or damage by an insurance policy effected by or for the seller, the purchase price is to be abated by the amount of that reduction.

5.1.2 If the contract provides that the policy insuring the property against loss or damage effected by or for the seller should continue in force after exchange of contracts, the seller is to:

(a) do everything required to continue to maintain the policy, including to pay promptly any premium which falls due

(b) increase the amount or extent of the cover as requested by the buyer, if the insurers agree and the buyer pays the additional premium

(c) permit the buyer to inspect the policy, or evidence of its terms, at any time
(d) obtain or consent to an endorsement on the policy of the buyer's interest, at the buyer's expense
(e) pay to the buyer immediately on receipt, any part of an additional premium which the buyer paid and which is returned by the insurers
(f) if before completion the property suffers loss or damage:
  (i) pay to the buyer on completion the amount of policy moneys which the seller has received; and
  (ii) if no final payment has then been received, assign to the buyer, at the buyer's expense, all rights to claim under the policy in such form as the buyer reasonably requires; and pending execution of the assignment, hold any policy moneys received in trust for the buyer

and the buyer is to pay the seller a proportionate part of the premium which the seller paid in respect of the period from the date when the contract is made to the date of actual completion.

5.1.3 (a) The following provisions apply if any part of the property transferred is subject to a lease.
(b) On completion the seller is to cancel the insurance policy relating to the property.
(c) The seller is to pay the buyer immediately on receipt the amount of the refund of premium received which relates to any part of the premium which was paid or reimbursed by a tenant or third party.
(d) The buyer is to hold the money paid subject to the rights of that tenant or third party.

5.1.4 Section 47 of the Law of Property Act 1925 does not apply.

5.2 Occupation by buyer

5.2.1 If the buyer is not already lawfully in the property, and the seller agrees to let the buyer into occupation, the following terms apply.

5.2.2 The buyer is a licensee and not a tenant. The terms of the licence are that the buyer:
(a) cannot transfer it
(b) is to pay or indemnify the seller against all outgoings and other expenses in respect of the property
(c) is to pay the seller a fee calculated at the contract rate on the purchase price (less any deposit paid) for the period of the licence
(d) is entitled to any rents and profits from any part of the property which the buyer does not occupy
(e) is to keep the property in as good a state of repair as it was in when the buyer went into occupation (except for fair wear and tear) and is not to alter it
(f) is not to infringe a statutory requirement relating to it
(g) is to quit the property when the licence ends.

5.2.3 The licence ends on the earliest of: completion date, rescission of the contract or when five working days' notice given by one party to the other takes effect.

5.2.4 If the buyer is in occupation of the property after the licence has come to an end and the contract is subsequently completed the buyer is to pay the seller compensation for its continued occupation calculated at the same rate as the fee mentioned in condition 5.2.2(c).

5.2.5 The buyer's right to raise requisitions is unaffected.

6. COMPLETION

6.1 Date

6.1.1 Completion date is twenty working days after the date of the contract but time is not of the essence of the contract unless a notice to complete has been served.

6.1.2 If the money due on completion is received after 2.00 p.m., completion is to be treated, for the purposes only of conditions 6.3 and 7.3, as taking place on the next working day.

6.2 Place

Completion is to take place in England and Wales, either at the seller's solicitor's office or at some other place which the seller reasonably specifies.

6.3 Apportionments

6.3.1 Subject to condition 6.3.7 income and outgoings of the property are to be apportioned between the parties so far as the change of ownership on completion will affect entitlement to receive or liability to pay them.

6.3.2 If the whole property is sold with vacant possession or the seller exercises its option in condition 7.3.4, apportionment is to be made with effect from the date of actual completion; otherwise, it is to be made from completion date.

6.3.3 In apportioning any sum, it is to be assumed that the buyer owns the property from the beginning of the day on which the apportionment is to be made.

6.3.4 A sum to be apportioned is to be treated as accruing:
(a) from day to day throughout the period for which it is payable or receivable, even if it is payable by instalments, and
(b) at the rate from time to time applicable during the period for which the apportionment is made.

6.3.5 When a sum to be apportioned is not known or easily ascertainable at completion, a provisional apportionment is to be made according to the best estimate available. As soon as the amount is known, a final apportionment is to be made and notified to the other party. Any resulting balance is to be paid no more than ten working days later, and if not then paid the balance is to bear interest at the contract rate from then until payment.

6.3.6 Compensation payable under condition 5.2.4 is not to be apportioned.

6.3.7 This provision applies where any lease subject to which the property is sold obliges the tenant to pay a service charge.
(a) On completion the buyer is to pay the seller the amount of any service charge expenditure already incurred by the seller but not yet due from the tenant.
(b) On completion the seller is to credit the buyer with service charge payments already recovered from the tenant but not yet incurred by the seller.

6.3.8 Condition 6.3.9 applies if:
(a) any part of the property is sold subject to a lease
(b) on completion any rent or service charge payable under the lease is due but not paid
(c) the contract does not provide that the buyer is to assign to the seller the right to collect any arrears due to the seller under the terms of the contract, and
(d) the seller is not entitled to recover any arrears from the tenant.

6.3.9 (a) The buyer is to seek to collect all the arrears in the ordinary course of management, but need not take legal proceedings or distrain
(b) A payment made on account of arrears is to be apportioned between the parties in the ratio of the sums owed to each, unless the tenant exercises its right to appropriate the payment in some other manner
(c) Any part of a payment on account of arrears received by one party but due to the other is to be paid no more than ten working days after the receipt of cash or cleared funds and, if not then paid, the sum is to bear interest at the contract rate until payment.

6.4 Amount payable

The amount payable by the buyer on completion is the purchase price (less any deposit already paid to the seller or its agent) adjusted to take account of:
(a) apportionments made under condition 6.3
(b) any compensation to be paid under condition 7.3
(c) any sum payable under condition 5.1.2.

6.5 Title deeds

6.5.1 As soon as the buyer has complied with all its obligations on completion the seller must part with the documents of title.

6.5.2 Condition 6.5.1 does not apply to any documents of title relating to land being retained by the seller after completion.

6.6 Rent receipts

The buyer is to assume that whoever gave any receipt for a payment of rent or service charge which the seller produces was the person or the agent of the person then entitled to that rent or service charge.

6.7 Means of payment

The buyer is to pay the money due on completion by direct credit and by an unconditional release of any deposit held by a stakeholder.

6.8 Notice to complete

6.8.1 At any time on or after the completion date, a party who is ready, able and willing to complete may give the other a notice to complete.

6.8.2 A party is ready, able and willing:
(a) if it could be, but for the default of the other party, and
(b) in the case of the seller, even though a mortgage remains secured on the property, if the amount to be paid on completion enables the property to be transferred freed of all mortgages (except those to which the sale is expressly subject).

6.8.3 The parties are to complete the contract within ten working days of giving a notice to complete, excluding the day on which the notice is given. For this purpose, time is of the essence of the contract.

6.8.4 On receipt of a notice to complete:
(a) if the buyer paid no deposit, it is forthwith to pay a deposit of 10 per cent
(b) if the buyer paid a deposit of less than 10 per cent, it is forthwith to pay a further deposit equal to the balance of that 10 per cent.

7 REMEDIES

7.1 Errors and omissions

7.1.1 If any plan or statement in the contract, or in the negotiations leading to it, is or was misleading or inaccurate due to an error or omission, the remedies available are as follows.

7.1.2 When there is a material difference between the description or value of the property as represented and as it is, the injured party is entitled to damages.

7.1.3 An error or omission only entitles the injured party to rescind the contract:
(a) where that error or omission results from fraud or recklessness, or
(b) where that party would be obliged, to its prejudice, to transfer or accept property differing substantially (in quantity, quality or tenure) from that which the error or omission had led it to expect.

7.2 Rescission

If either party rescinds the contract:
(a) unless the rescission is a result of the buyer's breach of contract the deposit is to be repaid to the buyer with accrued interest
(b) the buyer is to return any documents received from the seller and is to cancel any registration of the contract
(c) the seller's duty to pay any returned premium under condition 5.1.2(e) (whenever received) is not affected.

7.3 Late completion

7.3.1 If the buyer defaults in performing its obligations under the contract and completion is delayed, the buyer is to pay compensation to the seller.

7.3.2 Compensation is calculated at the contract rate on the purchase price (less any deposit paid) for the period between completion date and actual completion, but ignoring any period during which the seller was in default.

7.3.3 Any claim by the seller for loss resulting from delayed completion is to be reduced by any compensation paid under this contract.

7.3.4 Where the sale is not with vacant possession of the whole property and completion is delayed, the seller may give notice to the buyer, before the date of actual completion, that it will take the net income from the property until completion as well as compensation under condition 7.3.1.

7.4 After completion

Completion does not cancel liability to perform any outstanding obligation under the contract.

7.5 Buyer's failure to comply with notice to complete

7.5.1 If the buyer fails to complete in accordance with a notice to complete, the following terms apply.

7.5.2 The seller may rescind the contract, and if it does so:
(a) it may
  (i) forfeit and keep any deposit and accrued interest
  (ii) resell the property
  (iii) claim damages
(b) the buyer is to return any documents received from the seller and is to cancel any registration of the contract.

7.5.3 The seller retains its other rights and remedies.

7.6 Seller's failure to comply with notice to complete

7.6.1 If the seller fails to complete in accordance with a notice to complete, the following terms apply.

7.6.2 The buyer may rescind the contract, and if it does so:
(a) the deposit is to be repaid to the buyer with accrued interest
(b) the buyer is to return any documents it received from the seller and is, at the seller's expense, to cancel any registration of the contract.

7.6.3 The buyer retains its other rights and remedies.

8. LEASEHOLD PROPERTY

8.1 Existing leases

8.1.1 The following provisions apply to a sale of leasehold land.

8.1.2 The seller having provided the buyer with copies of the documents embodying the lease terms, the buyer is treated as entering into the contract knowing and fully accepting those terms.

8.1.3 The seller is to comply with any lease obligations requiring the tenant to insure the property.

8.2 New leases

8.2.1 The following provisions apply to a grant of a new lease.

8.2.2 The conditions apply so that:
"seller" means the proposed landlord
"buyer" means the proposed tenant
"purchase price" means the premium to be paid on the grant of a lease.

8.2.3 The lease is to be in the form of the draft attached to the contract.

8.2.4 If the term of the new lease will exceed 21 years, the seller is to deduce a title which will enable the buyer to register the lease at HM Land Registry with an absolute title.

8.2.5 The seller may not be required to grant a lease to any person other than the buyer.

8.2.6 The seller is to engross the lease and a counterpart of it and is to send the counterpart to the buyer at least five working days before completion date.

8.2.7 The buyer is to execute the counterpart and deliver it to the seller on completion.

8.3 Landlord's consent

8.3.1 The following provisions apply if the property is leasehold and the terms of the lease require a reversioner whether or not immediate (a "landlord") to consent to an assignment or sub-letting.

8.3.2 The seller is to:
(a) apply for the consent at its expense, and to use all reasonable efforts to obtain it
(b) give the buyer notice forthwith on obtaining the consent
(c) enter into an authorised guarantee agreement if the lease so requires.

8.3.3 Where the landlord lawfully requires, the buyer is to:
(a) use reasonable endeavours to provide promptly all information and references
(b) covenant directly with the landlord to observe the tenant's covenants and the conditions in the seller's lease
(c) use reasonable endeavours to provide guarantees of the performance and observance of the tenant's covenants and the conditions in the seller's lease
(d) execute or procure the execution of the licence.

8.3.4 If the landlord's consent has not been obtained by the original completion date:
(a) the time for completion is to be postponed until five working days after the seller gives written notice to the buyer that the consent has been obtained or four months from the original completion date whichever is the earlier
(b) the postponed date is to be treated as the completion date.

8.3.5 At any time after four months from the original completion date, either party may rescind the contract by notice to the other if:
(a) consent has still not been given, and
(b) no declaration has been obtained from the court that consent has been unreasonably withheld.

8.3.6 Neither party may object to a consent subject to a condition:
(a) which under section 19(1A) of the Landlord and Tenant Act 1927 is not regarded as unreasonable,
(b) which is lawfully imposed under an express term of the lease.

8.3.7 If the contract is rescinded under condition 8.3.5 the seller is to remain liable for any breach of condition 8.3.2 and the buyer is to remain liable for any breach of condition 8.3.3 but in all other respects neither party is to be treated as in breach of contract and condition 7.2. applies.

8.3.8 A party in breach of its obligations under condition 8.3.2 or 8.3.3 cannot rescind under condition 8.3.5 for so long as its breach is a cause of the consent's being withheld.

9. CHATTELS

9.1 The following provisions apply to any chattels which are to be sold.

9.2 Whether or not a separate price is to be paid for the chattels, the contract takes effect as a contract for sale of goods.

9.3 Ownership of the chattels passes to the buyer on actual completion but they are at the buyer's risk from the contract date.

SPECIAL CONDITIONS

1. This Contract incorporates the Standard Commercial Property Conditions (First Edition). Where there is a conflict between those Conditions and any other provision of this Contract, that other provision prevails.

2. The Property is sold subject to the Incumbrances on the Property and the Buyer will raise no requisition on them.

3. The Property is sold with vacant possession on completion.

(or) 3. The Property is sold subject to the following leases or tenancies:

4. The chattels at the Property and set out on the attached list are included in the sale.

Seller's Solicitors   :

Buyer's Solicitors   :

Property Information Form – Part I

Address of the Property:

Hatherleigh Farmhouse Saxmundham Road Framlingham Woodbridge
Suffolk IP13 9PH

IMPORTANT NOTE TO SELLERS

* **Please complete this form carefully. It will be sent to the buyer's solicitor and may be seen by the buyer. If you are unsure how to answer any of the questions, ask your solicitor before doing so.**

* For many of the questions you need only tick the correct answer. Where necessary, please give more detailed answers on a separate sheet of paper. Then send all the replies to your solicitor so that the information can be passed to the buyer's solicitor.

* The answers should be those of the person whose name is on the deeds. If there is more than one of you, you should prepare the answers together.

* It is very important that your answers are correct because the buyer will rely on them in deciding whether to go ahead. Incorrect information given to the buyer through your solicitor, or mentioned to the buyer in conversation between you, may mean that the buyer can claim compensation from you or even refuse to complete the purchase.

* It does not matter if you do not know the answer to any question so long as you say so.

* The buyer will be told by his solicitor that he takes the property as it is. If he wants more information about it, he should get it from his own advisers, not from you.

* If anything changes after you fill in this questionnaire but before the sale is completed, tell your solicitor immediately. This is as important as giving the right answers in the first place.

* Please pass to your solicitor immediately any notices you have received which affect the property. The same goes for notices which arrive at any time before completion.

* If you have a tenant, tell your solicitor immediately there is any change in the arrangements but do nothing without asking your solicitor first.

* You should let your solicitor have any letters, agreements or other documents which help answer the questions. If you know of any which you are not supplying with these answers, please tell your solicitor about them.

* Please complete and return the separate Fixtures, Fittings and Contents Form. It is an important document which will form part of the contract between you and the buyer. Unless you mark clearly on it the items which you wish to remove, they will be included in the sale and you will not be able to take them with you when you move.

Part I – to be completed by the seller

1   Boundaries

"Boundaries" mean any fence, wall,
hedge or ditch which marks the edge of
your property.

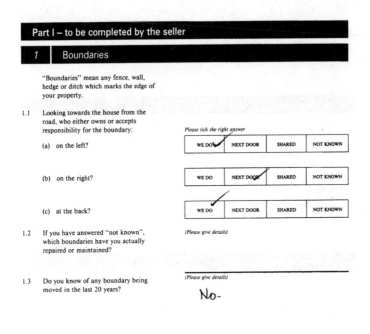

1.1   Looking towards the house from the
road, who either owns or accepts
responsibility for the boundary:

Please tick the right answer

(a)   on the left?

| WE DO ✓ | NEXT DOOR | SHARED | NOT KNOWN |

(b)   on the right?

| WE DO | NEXT DOOR ✓ | SHARED | NOT KNOWN |

(c)   at the back?

| WE DO | NEXT DOOR | SHARED | NOT KNOWN |

1.2   If you have answered "not known",
which boundaries have you actually
repaired or maintained?

(Please give details)

1.3   Do you know of any boundary being
moved in the last 20 years?

(Please give details)

No-

2   Disputes

2.1   Do you know of any disputes about
this or any neighbouring property?

| NO ✓ | YES: (PLEASE GIVE DETAILS) |

2.2   Have you received any complaints
about anything you have, or have not,
done as owners?

| NO ✓ | YES: (PLEASE GIVE DETAILS) |

Please tick the right answer

2.3   Have you made any such complaints to any
neighbour about what the neighbour has or has
not done?

NO	YES: (PLEASE GIVE DETAILS)

3 | Notices

3.1   Have you either sent or received any letters or
notices which affect your property or the
neighbouring property in any way (for example,
from or to neighbours, the council or a
government department)?

NO	YES	COPY ENCLOSED	TO FOLLOW	LOST

3.2   Have you had any negotiations or discussions
with any neighbour or any local or other
authority which affect the property in any way?

NO	YES: (PLEASE GIVE DETAILS)

4 | Guarantees

4.1   Are there any guarantees or insurance policies of
the following types:

(a)   NHBC Foundation 15 or Newbuild?

NO	YES	COPIES ENCLOSED	WITH DEEDS	LOST

(b)   Damp course?

NO	YES	COPIES ENCLOSED	WITH DEEDS	LOST

(c)   Double glazing?

NO	YES	COPIES ENCLOSED	WITH DEEDS	LOST

(d)   Electrical work?

NO	YES	COPIES ENCLOSED	WITH DEEDS	LOST

(e)   Roofing?

NO	YES	COPIES ENCLOSED	WITH DEEDS	LOST

(f)   Rot or infestation?

NO	YES	COPIES ENCLOSED	WITH DEEDS	LOST

(g)   Central heating?

NO	YES	COPIES ENCLOSED	WITH DEEDS	LOST

(h)   Anything similar? (e.g. cavity wall
insulation)

NO	YES	COPIES ENCLOSED	WITH DEEDS	LOST

(i)   Do you have written details of the work
done to obtain any of these guarantees?

NO	YES	COPIES ENCLOSED	WITH DEEDS	LOST

Please tick the right answer

4.2   Have you made or considered making claims under any of these?

NO ✓	YES: (PLEASE GIVE DETAILS)

---

5   Services

(This section applies to gas, electrical and water supplies, sewerage disposal and telephone cables.)

5.1   Please tick which services are connected to the property?

GAS ✓	ELEC. ✓	WATER ✓	DRAINS	TEL. ✓	CABLE T.V.

5.2   Do any drains, pipes or wires for these cross any neighbour's property?

NOT KNOWN ✓	YES: (PLEASE GIVE DETAILS)

5.3   Do any drains, pipes or wires leading to any neighbour's property cross your property?

NOT KNOWN ✓	YES: (PLEASE GIVE DETAILS)

5.4   Are you aware of any agreement which is not with the deeds about any of these services?

NOT KNOWN ✓	YES: (PLEASE GIVE DETAILS)

---

6   Sharing with the neighbours

6.1   Are you aware of any responsibility to contribute to the cost of anything used jointly, such as the repair of a shared drive, boundary or drain?

YES: (PLEASE GIVE DETAILS) ✓	NO

Shared driveway

Please tick the right answer

6.2 Do you contribute to the cost of repair of anything used by the neighbourhood, such as the maintenance of a private road?

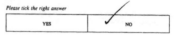

6.3 If so, who is responsible for organising the work and collecting the contributions?

6.4 Please give details of all such sums paid or owing, and explain if they are paid on a regular basis or only as and when work is required.

6.5 Do you need to go next door if you have to repair or decorate your building or maintain any of the boundaries?

t 6 If "Yes", have you always been able to do so without objection by the neighbours?

6.7 Do any of your neighbours need to come onto your land to repair or decorate their building or maintain the boundaries?

6.8 If so, have you ever objected?

7 │ Arrangements and rights

Are there any other formal or informal arrangements which give someone else rights over your property?

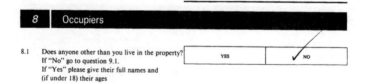

8 │ Occupiers

8.1 Does anyone other than you live in the property? If "No" go to question 9.1. If "Yes" please give their full names and (if under 18) their ages

Please tick the right answer

8.2 (a)(i) Do any of them have any right to stay on the property without your permission?

(These rights may have arisen without you realising, e.g. if they have paid towards the cost of buying the house, paid for improvements or helped you make your mortgage payments)

NO	YES: (PLEASE GIVE DETAILS)

8.2 (a)(ii) Are any of them tenants or lodgers?

NO	YES: (PLEASE GIVE DETAILS AND A COPY OF ANY TENANCY AGREEMENT)

8.2 (b) Have they all agreed to sign the contract for sale agreeing to leave with you (or earlier)?

NO	YES: (PLEASE GIVE DETAILS)

9 | Restrictions

If you have changed the use of the property or carried out any building work on it, please read the note below and answer these questions. If you have not, please go on to Question 10.

Note The title deeds of some properties include clauses which are called "restrictive covenants". For example, these may forbid the owner of the house to carry out any building work or to use it for the purpose of a business – unless someone else (often the builder of the house) gives his consent.

9.1 (a) Do you know of any "restrictive covenant" which applies to your house or land?

NO ✓	YES

(b) If "Yes" did you ask for consent for the work or change of use?

NO	YES: (PLEASE GIVE DETAILS AND A COPY OF ANY CONSENT)

9.2 If consent was needed but not obtained, please explain why not.

9.3 If the reply to 9.1(a) is "Yes", please give the
name and address of the person from whom
consent has to be obtained.

10 | Planning

10.1 Is the property used only as a private home?

Please tick the right answer

YES	NO: (PLEASE GIVE DETAILS)

10.2(a) Is the property a listed building or in a
conservation area?

YES	NO ✓	NOT KNOWN

(b) If "Yes", what work has been carried out since
it was listed or the area became a conservation
area?

10.3(a) Has there been any building work on the
property in the last four years?

NO ✓	YES: (PLEASE GIVE DETAILS)

(b) If "Yes", was planning permission, building
regulation approval or listed building consent
obtained?

NO	NOT REQUIRED	YES:	COPIES ENCLOSED	TO FOLLOW	LOST

10.4 Have you applied for planning permission,
building regulation approval or listing building
consent at any time?

NO ✓	YES:	COPIES ENCLOSED	TO FOLLOW	LOST

10.5 If "Yes", has any of the work been carried out?

NO	YES: (PLEASE GIVE DETAILS)

10.6(a) Has there been any change of use of the
property in the last ten years (e.g. dividing into
flats, combining flats or using part for business
use)?

NO ✓	YES: (PLEASE GIVE DETAILS)

(b) If "Yes", was planning permission obtained?

NO	NOT REQUIRED	YES:	COPIES ENCLOSED	TO FOLLOW	LOST

11 Fixtures

Please tick the right answer

11.1 If you have sold through an estate agent, are all items listed in its particulars included in the sale?

YES ✓	NO

If "No" you should instruct the estate agent to write to everyone concerned correcting this error.

11.2 Do you own outright everything included in the sale?

YES ✓	NO: (PLEASE GIVE DETAILS)

(You must give details of anything which may not be yours to sell, for example, anything rented or on H.P.)

12 Expenses

Have you ever had to pay for the use of the property?

NO ✓	YES: (PLEASE GIVE DETAILS)

(Ignore rates, water rates, council tax and gas, electricity and phone bills. Disclose anything else: examples are the clearance of cess pool or septic tank, drainage rate, rent charge.)

13 General

Is there any other information which you think the buyer may have a right to know?

NO ✓	YES: (PLEASE GIVE DETAILS)

Signature(s) ....

....

Date ....12 · 07 · 96...........................

Prop 1/8

This form is part of The Law Society's TransAction scheme © The Law Society 1994.
The Law Society is the professional body for solicitors in England and Wales.
The Solicitors' Law Stationery Society Ltd, Oyez House, 7 Spa Road, London SE16 3QQ

OYEZ 3.95 F29328
5065062

THE LAW SOCIETY

Prop 1

Property Information Form – Part II

SELLER'S PROPERTY INFORMATION FORM

Part II – to be completed by the seller's solicitor and to be sent with Part I

Address of the Property:

> Hatherleigh Farmhouse Saxmundham Road Framlingham Woodbridge
> Suffolk IP13 9PH

A	Boundaries

Does the information in the deeds agree with the seller's reply to 1.1 in Part I?

Please tick the right answer

YES ✓   NO (PLEASE GIVE DETAILS)

B	Relevant Documents

Are you aware of any correspondence, notices, consents or other documents other than those disclosed in Questions 3 or 4 of Part I?

YES   ✓ NO

C	Guarantees

If appropriate, have guarantees been assigned to the seller and notice of an assignment given?

YES   ✓ NO   NOT KNOWN

If "Yes", please supply copies, including copies of all guarantees not enclosed with Part I of this Form.

D	Services

Please give full details of all legal rights enjoyed to ensure the benefit of uninterrupted services, e.g. easements, wayleaves, licences, etc.

As disclosed by office copy entries.

E | Adverse Interests

Please give full details of all overriding interests affecting the property as defined by the Land Registration Act 1925, s.70(1).

None to our knowledge

F | Restrictions

Who has the benefit of any restrictive covenants? If known, please provide the name and address of the person or company having such benefit or the name and address of his or its solicitors.

Not known.

G | Mechanics of Sale

Please tick the right answer

(a) Is this sale dependent on the seller buying another property?

YES ✓	NO

(b) If "Yes", what stage have the negotiations reached?

Same as this

(c) Does the seller require a mortgage?

YES	✓ NO

(d) If "Yes", has an offer been received and/or accepted or a mortgage certificate obtained?

YES	NO

H | Deposit

Will the whole or part of the deposit be used on a related transaction?

NO	✓ YES (PLEASE GIVE DETAILS)

If so, please state to whom it will be paid and in what capacity it will be held by them.

To be agreed

Seller's Solicitor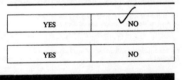

Date........12....07....46........

Reminder
1. The Fixtures, Fittings and Contents Form should be supplied in addition to the information above.
2. Copies of all planning permissions, buildings regulations consents, guarantees, assignments and notices should be supplied with this form.
3. If the property is leasehold, also complete the Seller's Leasehold Information Form.

Prop 2/2

This form is part of The Law Society's TransAction scheme © The Law Society 1994.
The Law Society is the professional body for solicitors in England and Wales.
The Solicitors' Law Stationery Society Ltd, Oyez House, 7 Spa Road, London SE16 3QQ

OYEZ 4.95 F29499
5065063
* * *

THE LAW SOCIETY

Prop 2

Leasehold Property Information Form – Part I

Address of the Property:

> Hatherleigh Farmhouse   Saxmundham Road   Framlingham   Woodbridge
> Suffolk   IP13 9DR

If you live in leasehold property, please answer the following questions. Some people live in blocks of flats, others in large houses converted into flats and others in single leasehold houses. These questions cover all types of leasehold property, but some of them may not apply to your property. In that case please answer them N/A.

The instructions set out at the front of the Seller's Property Information Form apply to this form as well. Please read them again before giving your answers to these questions.

If you are unsure how to answer any of the questions, ask your solicitor.

Part I – to be completed by the seller

1 | Management Company

1.1 If there is a management company which is run by the tenants please supply any of the following documents which are in your possession:

Please mark the appropriate box

(a) Memorandum and articles of association of the company.

ENCLOSED ✓	TO FOLLOW	LOST	N/A

(b) Your share or membership certificate.

ENCLOSED ✓	TO FOLLOW	LOST	N/A

(c) The management accounts for the last 3 years.

ENCLOSED	TO FOLLOW ✓	LOST	N/A

(d) Copy of any regulations made by either the landlord or the company additional to the rules contained in the lease.

ENCLOSED ✓	TO FOLLOW	LOST	N/A

(e) The names and addresses of the secretary and treasurer of the company.

2 | The Landlord

2.1 What is the name and address of your landlord?

_____

2.2 If the landlord employs an agent to collect the
rent, what is the name and address of that agent?

_____

2.3 Do you have the landlord's receipt for the last
rent payment?

YES ✓ (Please tick box and send it with these answers)

NO: (Explain why not)

_____

2.4 Do you pay a share of the maintenance costs of
the building?

YES ✓ (Please tick box and send the receipt, or demand, for the last
payment with these answers)

NO: (Explain why not)

_____

3 | Maintenance Charges

3.1 Do you know of any unusual expense likely to
show in the maintenance charge accounts in the
next year or two?

If "Yes", please give details.

Please mark the appropriate box

YES ✓	NO

Roof repairs.

3.2 How much have you paid for maintenance
charges in each of the last 3 years?

£500 p.a.

3.3 Do you have the receipts for these?

NO	✓ YES	ENCLOSED	TO FOLLOW	LOST

Prop 4/2

Please mark the appropriate box

3.4 Do you know of any problems in the last 3 years between flat owners and the landlord or maintenance company about maintenance charges, or the method of management?

If "Yes", please give details.

YES	NO ✓

3.5 Have you challenged the maintenance charge or any expense in the last 3 years?

If "Yes", please give details.

YES	NO ✓

3.6 Do you know if the landlord has had any problems in collecting the maintenance charges from other flat owners?

If "Yes", please give details.

YES	NO ✓

4   Notices

A landlord may serve a notice on a printed form or in the form of a letter and your buyer will wish to know if anything of this sort has been received.

4.1 Have you had a notice from the landlord that he wants to sell his interest in the building?

NO ✓	YES	COPY ENCLOSED	TO FOLLOW	LOST

4.2 Have you had any other notice or letter about the building, its use, its condition or its repair and maintenance?

NO ✓	YES	COPY ENCLOSED	TO FOLLOW	LOST

5   Consents

Are you aware of any changes in the terms of the lease or of the landlord giving any consents under the lease? (This may be in a deed, a letter or even verbal.) If not in writing, please supply details.

NO ✓	NOT KNOWN	YES	COPIES ENCLOSED	TO FOLLOW	LOST

6   Complaints

6.1 Have you received any complaints from the landlord, any landlord above him, management company or any other tenant about anything you have or have not done?

If "Yes", please give details.

YES	NO ✓

Please mark the appropriate box

6.2 Have you had cause for complaint to any of them?

YES	✓ NO

If "Yes", please give details.

6.3 Have you complained to anyone else about the conduct of any other occupier?

YES	✓ NO

If "Yes", please give details.

7 Insurance

7.1 Do you have to arrange the insurance on the building?

YES	✓ NO

If "No", go to Question 7.4

7.2 If "Yes", do you have a copy of the insurance policy?

COPY ENCLOSED	TO FOLLOW	LOST

7.3 Do you have a copy of the receipt for the last payment of the premium?

COPY ENCLOSED	TO FOLLOW	LOST

7.4 Do you have a copy of the insurance policy arranged by the landlord or the management company and a copy of the schedule for the current year?

NO	YES	COPIES ENCLOSED	TO FOLLOW	LOST

8 Decoration

8.1 If outside decoration is your responsibility, when was it last done?

IN THE YEAR 19 89	NOT KNOWN

9 | Alterations

Please mark the appropriate box

9.1 Are you aware of any alterations having been made to your property since the lease was originally granted?

YES	NO ✓	NOT KNOWN

If "Yes", please supply details.

9.2 If "Yes", was the landlord's consent obtained?

NO	NOT KNOWN	NOT REQUIRED	YES	COPIES ENCLOSED	TO FOLLOW	LOST

10 | Occupation

10.1 Are you now occupying the property as your sole or main home?

YES ✓	NO

10.2 Have you occupied the property as your sole or main home (apart from usual holidays and business trips) –

(a) continuously throughout the last twelve months?

YES ✓	NO

(b) continuously throughout the last three years?

YES ✓	NO

(c) for periods totalling at least three years during the last ten years?

YES	NO

11 | Enfranchisement

11.1 Have you served on your immediate or superior landlord a formal notice under the enfranchisement legislation stating your desire to buy the freehold or be granted an extended lease?

NO ✓	YES	COPY ENCLOSED	COPY TO FOLLOW	COPY LOST

If so, please supply a copy.

Please mark the appropriate box

11.2 If the property is a flat in a block, have you served on the immediate or any superior landlord any formal notices under the enfranchisement legislation relating to the possible collective purchase of the freehold of the block or part of it?

If so, please supply a copy.

NO ✓	YES	COPY ENCLOSED	COPY TO FOLLOW	COPY LOST

11.3 Has any letter or notice been served upon you in response?

NO ✓	YES	COPY ENCLOSED	COPY TO FOLLOW	COPY LOST

Signature(s): ....

Date: ....12.07.96........................

Prop 4/6

Leasehold Property Information Form – Part II

SELLER'S LEASEHOLD INFORMATION FORM

Part II – to be completed by the seller's solicitor and to be sent with Part I

Address of the Property:

Hatherleigh Farmhouse　Saxmundham Road　Framlingham　Woodbridge
Suffolk　IP13 9DR

A | Documents and Information

(1) In respect of any items not enclosed with Part I of this form, please supply copies or confirm that copies will be supplied in due course.

Please mark the appropriate box

	ENCLOSED	TO FOLLOW	N/A			ENCLOSED	TO FOLLOW	N/A
1.1(a) Memo and arts	✓			3.3 Receipt for service charge		✓		
1.1(b) Share cert	✓			4.2 Notices				✓
1.1(c) Accounts	✓			6.2 Seller's insurance	✓			
1.1(d) Regulations	✓			6.3 Seller's premium receipt		✓		
2.3 Rent receipt	✓			6.4 Landlord's insurance		✓		

(2) If apparent from the papers in your possession, please provide details of any names and addresses or other information that the seller was unable to provide on Part I of this form. Please state if any of that information will be supplied at a later date.

B | Landlord (including Management Company)

(1)　Please provide name and address of the recipient of notice of assignment and charge.

(2)　Do the insurers make a practice of recording the interest of the buyer's mortgagee and the buyer on the policy?

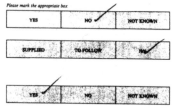

Please mark the appropriate box

YES	NO ✓	NOT KNOWN

(3)　Please supply a copy of the fire certificate.

SUPPLIED	TO FOLLOW	N/A ✓

(4)　How many flats are there in the building?

(5)　Are all of them let on identical leases? If not, in what respect do they differ?

YES ✓	NO	NOT KNOWN

(6) Has the landlord experienced problems with the collection of maintenance charges as they fall due?
If so, please supply details.

Please mark the appropriate box

| YES ✓ | NO | NOT KNOWN |

Details to follow.

C   Notices

(1) In respect of any items or information not enclosed with Part I of this form, please answer the following questions:

1(1) Please supply details of any notices served upon the seller under the Landlord and Tenant Act 1987 indicating that the landlord is proposing to sell the landlord's reversionary interest in the building.

1(2) Please state what is the present position as a result of the service of the notice.

| ENCLOSED | TO FOLLOW | N/A ✓ |

2(1) Please supply a copy of any Notice served by the seller under the Leasehold Reform Act 1967 or the Leasehold Reform Housing and Urban Development Act 1993.

| ENCLOSED | TO FOLLOW | N/A ✓ |

2(2) Please supply a copy of any letter or Notice served upon the seller in response.

| ENCLOSED | TO FOLLOW | N/A ✓ |

3(1) Please supply details of any notices served under Sections 18-30 Landlord and Tenant Act 1985.

3(2) Has the seller paid all contributions required by the notice?
If not, please state reasons.

| YES ✓ | NO |

D   House Conversions

If planning consent cannot be produced, please provide a copy of an established use certificate.
In the absence of either, please supply evidence of permitted use.

| ENCLOSED | TO FOLLOW | N/A ✓ |

Reminder
Copies of any relevant documents should be supplied with this Form.

Seller's Solicitor ....

Date .... 12 : 07 : 46 ....

Prop 5/2

This form is part of The Law Society's TransAction scheme © The Law Society 1994.
The Law Society is the professional body for solicitors in England and Wales.
The Solicitors' Law Stationery Society Ltd, Oyez House, 7 Spa Road, London SE16 3QQ

OYEZ   4.94 F27038
5065066

THE LAW SOCIETY   Prop 5

Fixtures, Fittings and Contents Form

FIXTURES FITTINGS AND CONTENTS (2ND EDITION)

Address of the Property:

Hatherleigh Farmhouse Saxmundham Road Framlingham
Woodbridge Suffolk IP13 9PH

1. Place a tick in one of these three columns against every item.

2. The second column ("excluded from the sale") is for items on the list which you are proposing to take with you when you move. If you are prepared to sell any of these to the buyer, please write the price you wish to be paid beside the name of the item and the buyer can then decide whether or not to accept your offer to sell.

	INCLUDED IN THE SALE	EXCLUDED FROM THE SALE	NONE AT THE PROPERTY
TV Aerial/Satellite Dish	✓		
Radio Aerial			✓
Immersion Heater	✓		
Hot Water Cylinder Jacket	✓		
Roof Insulation	✓		
Wall Heaters			✓
Night Storage Heater			✓
Gas/Electric Fires			✓
Light Fittings:			
Ceiling Lights	☑	☐	☐
Wall Lights	☑	☐	☐
Lamp Shades	☐	☑	☐
N.B. If these are to be removed, it is assumed that they will be replaced by ceiling rose and socket, flex, bulb holder and bulb.			
Switches	✓		
Electric Points	✓		
Dimmer Switches			✓

This form comprises 6 pages. Please ensure you complete all sections on all pages. Please turn over to the next page.

	INCLUDED IN THE SALE	EXCLUDED FROM THE SALE	NONE AT THE PROPERTY
Fluorescent Lighting			✓
Outside Lights	✓		
Telephone Receivers:			
British Telecom	☑	☐	☐
Own	☐	☑	☐
Burglar Alarm System			✓
Complete Central Heating System	✓		
Extractor Fans			✓
Doorbell/Chimes	✓		
Door Knocker	✓		
Door Furniture:			
Internal	☑	☐	☐
External	☑	☐	☐
Double Glazing	✓		
Window Fitments	✓		
Shutters/Grills			✓
Curtain Rails	✓		
Curtain Poles	✓		
Pelmets			✓
Venetian Blinds			✓
Roller Blinds			✓
Curtains (Including Net Curtains):			
Lounge	☐	☑	☐
Dining Room	☐	☑	☐

	INCLUDED IN THE SALE	EXCLUDED FROM THE SALE	NONE AT THE PROPERTY
Kitchen	☐	☑	☐
Bathroom	☐	☑	☐
Bedroom 1	☐	☑	☐
Bedroom 2	☐	☑	☐
Bedroom 3	☐	☑	☐
Bedroom 4	☐	☑	☐
Other Rooms (state which)			
1. STUDY	☐	☑	☐
2.	☐	☐	☐
3.	☐	☐	☐
Carpets and other Floor Covering:			
Lounge	☑	☐	☐
Dining Room	☐	☐	☑
Kitchen	☐	☐	☑
Hall, Stairs and Landing	☐	☐	☑
Bathroom	☑	☐	☐
Bedroom 1	☑	☐	☐
Bedroom 2	☑	☐	☐
Bedroom 3	☑	☐	☐
Bedroom 4			
Other Rooms (state which)			
1.	☐	☐	☐

	INCLUDED IN THE SALE	EXCLUDED FROM THE SALE	NONE AT THE PROPERTY
2.	☐	☐	☐
3.	☐	☐	☐
Storage Units in Kitchen			
Kitchen Fitments:			
Fitted Cupboards and Shelves	☑	☐	☐
Refrigerator/ Fridge-Freezer	☐	☑	☐
Oven	☑	☐	☐
Extractor Hood	☐	☐	☑
Hob	☑	☐	☐
Cutlery Rack	☐	☐	☑
Spice Rack	☐	☐	☑
Other (state which)			
1.	☐	☐	☐
2.	☐	☐	☐
3.	☐	☐	☐
Kitchen Furniture:			
Washing Machine	☐	☑	☐
Dishwasher	☐	☑	☐
Tumble-Drier	☐	☐	☑
Cooker	☑	☐	☐
Other (state which)			
1.	☐	☐	☐

	INCLUDED IN THE SALE	EXCLUDED FROM THE SALE	NONE AT THE PROPERTY
2.	☐	☐	☐
3.	☐	☐	☐
Bathroom Fitments:			
Cabinet	☐	☐	☑
Towel Rails	☑	☐	☐
Soap and Tooth-brush Holders	☐	☐	☑
Toilet Roll Holders	☑	☐	☐
Fitted Shelves/ Cupboards	☑	☐	☐
Other Sanitary Fittings	☑	☐	☐
Shower			✓
Shower Fittings			✓
Shower Curtain			✓
Bedroom Fittings:			
Shelves	☐	☐	☑
Fitted Wardrobes	☐	☐	☑
Fitted Cupboards	✓		
Fitted Shelving/ Cupboards	✓		
Fitted Units			✓
Wall Mirrors		✓	
Picture Hooks	✓		
Plant Holders			✓
Clothes Line			✓
Rotary Line	✓		

Please turn over to the next page. Prop 6/5

	INCLUDED IN THE SALE	EXCLUDED FROM THE SALE	NONE AT THE PROPERTY
Garden Shed	✓		
Greenhouse			✓
Garden Ornaments			✓
Trees, Plants and Shrubs	✓		
Garden Produce			✓
Stock of Oil/Solid Fuel/Propane Gas	✓		
Water Butts	✓		
Dustbins		✓	
Other			

Signed Seller(s):.... *P.A. Clr* ....

....

Prop 6/6

 6.95 F29700
5065067
**

THE LAW SOCIETY   **Prop 6**

Form K15

Form K15

Land Charges Act 1972

Payment of fee

Insert a cross (X) in this box if the fee is to be paid through a credit account (see Note 3 overleaf)

☒

APPLICATION FOR AN OFFICIAL SEARCH
NOT APPLICABLE TO REGISTERED LAND

Application is hereby made for an official search in the index to the registers kept pursuant to the Land Charges Act 1972 for any subsisting entries in respect of the under-mentioned particulars.

IMPORTANT: Please read the notes overleaf before completing this form

For Official Use only

STX			NAMES TO BE SEARCHED (Please use block letters and see Note 4 overleaf)	PERIOD OF YEARS (see Note 5 overleaf)	
				From	To
	Forename(s)		RODNEY STEVEN		
	SURNAME		CLAYTON	1985	1996
	Forename(s)		PATRICIA MARIA		
	SURNAME		CLAYTON	1985	1996
	Forename(s)				
	SURNAME				
	Forename(s)				
	SURNAME				
	Forename(s)				
	SURNAME				
	Forename(s)				
	SURNAME				

COUNTY (see Note 6 overleaf)   Suffolk

FORMER COUNTY

DESCRIPTION OF LAND (see Note 7 overleaf)

FORMER DESCRIPTION

Particulars of Applicant (see Notes 8, 9 and 10 overleaf)		Name and Address (including postcode) for despatch of certificate
KEY NUMBER	Name and address (including postcode)	(Leave blank if certificate is to be returned to applicant's address)
3753706	Ross Coates Solicitor 139 Main Road Kesgrave IPSWICH Suffolk IP5 7NP	

| Applicant's reference: RMC/C/CLAY | Date 12th July 1996 | FOR OFFICIAL USE ONLY |

Form K16

Form K16

Land Charges Act 1972

Payment of Fee

Insert a cross (X)
in this box
if the fee is
to be debited
to your credit
account.

| X |

(See Note 2 overleaf)

APPLICATION FOR AN OFFICIAL SEARCH
(BANKRUPTCY ONLY)

Application is hereby made for an official search in the index to the registers kept pursuant to the Land Charges Act 1972 in respect of the under-mentioned names for any subsisting entries of:

(i) petitions in bankruptcy in the register of pending actions

(ii) receiving orders in bankruptcy and bankruptcy orders in the register of writs and orders

(iii) deeds of arrangement in the register of deeds of arrangement

For Official Use only		
#		

IMPORTANT: Please read the notes overleaf before completing the form.

NAMES TO BE SEARCHED
(Please use block letters and see Note 3 overleaf)

Forename(s)	RODNEY STEVEN
SURNAME	CLAYTON
Forename(s)	PATRICIA MARIA
SURNAME	CLAYTON
Forename(s)	
SURNAME	
Forename(s)	
SURNAME	
Forename(s)	
SURNAME	
Forename(s)	
SURNAME	

Particulars of Applicant (see Notes 4, 5 and 6 overleaf)		Name and address (including postcode) for despatch of certificate (Leave blank if certificate is to be returned to applicant's address)
KEY NUMBER	Name and address (including postcode)	
3753706	Ross Coates Solicitor 139 Main Road Kesgrave IPSWICH Suffolk IP5 7NP	

Applicant's reference:	Date	FOR OFFICIAL USE ONLY
RMC/C/CLAY	12th July 1996	

Completion information and requisitions on title

COMPLETION INFORMATION AND REQUISITIONS ON TITLE

> **WARNING: Replies to Requisitions 4.2 and 6.2 are treated as a solicitor's undertaking.**

Property: Hatherleigh Farmhouse   Saxmundham Road   Framlingham   Woodbridge   Suffolk   IP13 9PH

Seller: CLAYTON

Buyer: GARRATT

1.   PROPERTY INFORMATION

Please confirm that the written information given by or on behalf of the Seller prior to exchange of contracts is complete and accurate. (This includes SPIF Parts I and II, SLIF Parts I and II, Replies to Pre-Contract enquiries and correspondence between us.)

1. Confirmed, subject as varied, if at all by subsequent correspondence.

2.   VACANT POSSESSION

2.1   If vacant possession is to be given on completion:–

    (a)   What arrangements will be made to hand over the keys?

    (b)   By what time will the Seller have vacated the property on the completion date?

2.(a) The parties should make arrangements direct.

(b)   Lunchtime.

2.2   If vacant possession is not being given, please confirm that an authority to the Tenant to pay the rent to the Buyer will be available at completion.

2.2   N/A

3.   DEEDS

3.1   Do you hold all the title deeds? If not, where are they?

3.1   Yes

3.2   Please list the deeds and documents to be handed over on completion.

3.2   As per the Epitome of Title

3.3   If the land/charge certificate is on deposit, what is the deposit number? If it is not on deposit and will not be handed over on completion, please put it on deposit now and supply the deposit number on completion.

3.3.   N/A

4.   COMPLETION

4.1   Will completion take place at your office? If not, where will it take place?

4.1   At our office.

4.2   If we wish to complete through the post, please confirm that the Law Society's Code for Completion by Post will apply.

4.2   Yes

5.   MONEY

5.1   Please state the exact amount payable on completion. If it is not just the balance purchase money, please provide copy receipts for any rent or service charge or other payments being apportioned.

5.1   The balance purchase moneys are payable on completion.

Either

5.2   Please give: 5.2 (a)   Lloyds Bank Plc

        (a) Name and address of your bank.

        (b) Sort Code.   (b)   30-94-55

        (c) Your Client Account Number to   (c)   082517502
             which monies are to be sent.

Or

5.3   State in whose favour a banker's draft should   5.3 Ross Coates
        be drawn.

6.   UNDERTAKINGS

> **WARNING:** A reply to this requisition is treated as an undertaking. Great care must be taken when answering this requisition.

6.1   Please list the mortgages or charges ('the Charges')   6.1 Barclays Bank Plc
        secured on the property which you will discharge on or
        before completion. (This includes repayment of any
        discount under the Housing Act 1985 Right to Buy.)

6.2   Do you undertake to discharge the Charges listed in
        6.1 on completion and to send to us Form 53s or the   6.2 Yes
        receipted charges as soon as received by you?

Buyer's Solicitor

Seller's Solicitor

Date ....12 th July 1996.................................   Date ....20 th July 1996...............................

> **WARNING:** These replies should be signed only by a person with authority to give undertakings on behalf of the firm.

ADDITIONAL REQUISITIONS

Prop 7/2

This form is part of The Law Society's TransAction scheme © The Law Society 1994.
The Law Society is the professional body for solicitors in England and Wales.
The Solicitors' Law Stationery Society Ltd. Oyez House, 7 Spa Road, London SE16 3QQ

THE LAW SOCIETY   **Prop 7**

OYEZ 7.95 F29962
5065069

Form 109

Application for **Office Copies of Register/Title Plan; a certificate in Form 102**	HM Land Registry	**Form** **109**

(Rule 2 Land Registration (Open Register) Rules 1991)

The Kingston Upon Hull District Land Registry
DX 26700
HULL 4

Please complete the numbered panels on this form in typescript or BLOCK LETTERS.
No covering letter is necessary.
Applications for office copies of specified documents must be made on Form 110.
Use one form per title.

For official use only

Record of Fees paid

Fee Debited £

1 Title Number (if known)		
	(Use one character per box)	
2 Flat No., if applicable	**Property Description**	
Postal number or description	Hatherleigh Farmhouse	
Name of road	Saxmundham Road	
Name of locality	Framlingham	
Town	WOODBRIDGE	
District or London Borough		
Administrative County		
Post code	IP13 9PH	

4   **PAYMENT OF FEE**

Please enter X in the appropriate box:–

☐ the Land Registry fee of £ [ ] accompanies this application,
or
☒ please debit the Credit Account mentioned below with the appropriate fee payable under the current Land Registration Fees Order.

FOR COMPLETION BY APPLICANTS WHO ARE CREDIT ACCOUNT HOLDERS

YOUR KEY NUMBER:–
| 1 | 2 | 3 | 4 | 5 | 6 |

YOUR REFERENCE:– (See over)

3 Application

xx We, Ross Coates

(enter here name and address of person or firm making the application)
of   139 Main Road   Kesgrave   Ipswich

Suffolk   IP5 7NP

apply for

☒ office copy(ies) of the **register** of the above mentioned property;

☐ office copy(ies) of the **title plan** of the above mentioned property;

☐ a certificate in Form 102 in which case, either:–

☐ an Estate Plan has been approved and the Plot Number is
or
☐ no Estate Plan has been approved and a certificate is to be issued in respect of the land shown
on the attached plan and copy.

5 Please enter X in the appropriate box:–

☒ I am, or act for, either the registered proprietor, or an intending purchaser or mortgagee.

☐ The above does not apply.

Note: This information is requested for statistical purposes only.

6 Where the title number is NOT quoted in Panel 1 please enter X in the appropriate box(es):–
As regards this property, I am interested in the
☒ Freehold estate.

☐ Leasehold estate.

7 In case there is an application for registration pending against the title, please enter X in the appropriate box:–

☐ I require an office copy back dated to the day prior to the receipt of that application,
or
☐ I require an office copy on completion of that application.

Signature of applicant:–   Date 12th July 1996   Daytime telephone No:– (01473) 621800

8 Reference   RMC/C/CLAYTON

Ross Coates
Solicitor
139 Main Road
Kesgrave
IPSWICH
Suffolk
IP13 9PH

Please enter above using BLOCK LETTERS the name and either address (including postcode) OR (if applicable) the DX number of the person to whom the office copies are to be sent.

Where you have requested that the fee be paid by Credit Account the appropriate fee has been debited.

Form 94A

Application by **Purchaser**[a] for
Official Search with priority
of the whole of the land in either a
registered title or a pending first
registration application

HM Land Registry

Form

94A

Land Registration (Official
Searches) Rules 1993

Kingston Upon Hull   District Land Registry[b]
DX 26700
HULL 4

Small raised letters in **bold** type refer to explanatory notes overleaf.

Please complete the numbered panels

1 **Title number** (one only per form) - enter the title number of the registered land or that allotted to the pending first registration.

2 **Registered proprietor(s) / Applicant(s) for first registration**[c] - enter FULL name(s) either of the registered proprietor(s) of the land in the above title **or** of the person(s) applying for first registration of the land specified in panel 8.

SURNAME / ~~COMPANY NAME~~   CLAYTON

FORENAME(S): RODNEY STEVEN

SURNAME / ~~COMPANY NAME~~   CLAYTON

FORENAME(S): PATRICIA MARIA

3 **Search from date** - for a search of a **registered title** enter in the box a date falling within (a) of the definition of search from date in rule 2(1).[d]
Note: If the date entered is not such a date the application may be rejected. In the case of a **pending first registration** search, enter the letters 'FR'.

12   MAY   1991

4 **Applicant(s)** - enter FULL name of each purchaser, **or** lessee **or** chargee.

Halifax Building Society

5 **Reason for application** - I certify that the applicant(s) intend(s) to:- (enter X in the appropriate box)

[ ] P purchase   [ ] L take a lease of   [X] C take a registered charge on

(enter X in the appropriate box)

[X] the **whole** of the land in the above registered title **or**

[ ] the **whole** of the land in the pending first registration application referred to above.

6 Enter the key number[e] (if any) and the name and (DX) address of the person lodging the application (**use BLOCK LETTERS**).

Key number: [1] [3] [4] [4] [5] [6] [ ]

Name: ROSS COATES

DX No: 124721   DX Exchange: MARTLESHAM HEATH

Address including postcode (if DX not used):

Reference:[f]

7 Enter, using BLOCK LETTERS, the name and either address (including postcode) OR (if applicable) the DX No and exchange of the person to whom the result is to be sent. (Leave blank if result is to be sent to the address in panel 6.)

Reference:[f]

8 **Property details**
Administrative area[g]
Suffolk : Suffolk Coastal
Address (including postcode) or short description:
Hatherleigh Farmhouse
Saxmundham Road
Framlingham
WOODBRIDGE Suffolk IP13 9PH

9 **Type of search** (enter X in the appropriate box)

[X] **Registered land search**
Application is made to ascertain whether any adverse entry[h] has been made in the register or day list since the date shown in panel 3 above.

[ ] **Pending first registration search**
Application is made to ascertain whether any adverse entry has been made in the day list since the date of the pending first registration application referred to above.

10   **PAYMENT OF FEE**[i]

Please enter X in the appropriate box.

[ ] The Land Registry fee of £ [   ] accompanies this application; or

[X] Please debit the Credit Account mentioned in panel 6 with the appropriate fee payable under the current Land Registration Fees Order.

Note: If the fee is not paid by either of the above methods the application may be rejected.

Signature

Date 12.7.96   Telephone (01473) 621800

Form TR1

**Transfer of whole
of registered title(s)**

HM Land Registry

TR1

(If you need more room than is provided for in a panel, use continuation sheet CS and staple to this form)

---

1. Stamp Duty

Place "X" in the box that applies and complete the box in the appropriate certificate.

☐ I/We hereby certify that this instrument falls within category ☐ in the Schedule to the Stamp Duty (Exempt Instruments) Regulations 1987

☐ It is certified that the transaction effected does not form part of a larger transaction or of a series of transactions in respect of which the amount or value or the aggregate amount or value of the consideration exceeds the sum of

£ _____

---

2. Title Number(s) of the Property *(leave blank if not yet registered)*

---

3. Property

If this transfer is made under section 37 of the Land Registration Act 1925 following a not-yet-registered dealing with part only of the land in a title, or is made under rule 72 of the Land Registration Rules 1925, include a reference to the last preceding document of title containing a description of the property.

---

4. Date

---

5. Transferor *(give full names and Company's Registered Number if any)*

---

6. Transferee **for entry on the register** *(Give full names and Company's Registered Number if any; for Scottish Co. Reg. Nos., use an SC prefix. For foreign companies give territory in which incorporated)*

Unless otherwise arranged with Land Registry headquarters, a certified copy of the transferee's constitution (in English or Welsh) will be required if it is a body corporate but is not a company registered in England and Wales or Scotland under the Companies Acts.

---

7. Transferee's intended **address(es) for service** in the U.K. *(including postcode)* for entry on the register

---

8. The Transferor transfers the property to the Transferee.

9. Consideration *(Place 'X' in the box that applies. State clearly the currency unit if other than sterling. If none of the boxes applies, insert an appropriate memorandum in the additional provisions panel.)*

☐ The Transferor has received from the Transferee for the property the sum of *(in words and figures)*

☐ *(insert other receipt as appropriate)*

☐ The Transfer is not for money or anything which has a monetary value

10. The Transferor transfers with *(place 'X' in the box which applies and add any modifications)*

☐ full title guarantee　　　　☐ limited title guarantee

---

1 1. Declaration of trust *Where there is more than one transferee, place 'X' in the appropriate box.*

☐ The transferees are to hold the property on trust for themselves as joint tenants.

☐ The transferees are to hold the property on trust for themselves as tenants in common in equal shares.

☐ The transferees are to hold the property *(complete as necessary)*

---

12. Additional Provision(s) *Insert here any required or permitted statement, certificate or application and any agreed covenants, declarations, etc.*

---

13. *The Transferors and all other necessary parties should execute this transfer as a deed using the space below. Forms of execution are given in Schedule 3 to the Land Registration Rules 1925. If the transfer contains transferees' covenants or declarations or contains an application by them (e.g. for a restriction), it must also be executed by the Transferees.*

Signed as a Deed by the said:

in the presence of:

Signed as a Deed by the said:

in the presence of:

Signed as a Deed by the said:

in the presence of:

Form TP1

**Transfer of part
of registered title(s)**

HM Land Registry

TP1

(If you need more room than is provided for in a panel, use continuation sheet CS and staple to this form)

---

1. Stamp Duty

Place 'X' in the box that applies and complete the box in the appropriate certificate.

☐ It is certified that this instrument falls within category ☐ in the Schedule to the Stamp Duty (Exempt Instruments) Regulations 1987

☐ It is certified that the transaction effected does not form part of a larger transaction or of a series of transactions in respect of which the amount or value or the aggregate amount or value of the consideration exceeds the sum of

£

---

2. Title number(s) out of which the Property is transferred *(leave blank if not yet registered)*

---

3. Other title number(s) against which matters contained in this transfer are to be registered *(if any)*

---

4. Property transferred *(Insert address, including postcode, or other description of the property transferred. Any physical exclusions. e.g. mines and minerals, should be defined. Any attached plan must be signed by the transferor and by or on behalf of the transferee).*

The Property is defined: *(place "X" in the box that applies and complete the statement)*

☐ on the attached plan and shown *(state reference e.g. "edged red")*

☐ on the Transferor's filed plan(s) and shown *(state reference e.g. "edged and numbered 1 in blue")*

---

5. Date

---

6. Transferor *(give full names and Company's Registered Number if any)*

---

7. Transferee for entry on the register *(Give full names and Company's Registered Number if any; for Scottish Co. Reg. Nos., use an SC prefix. For foreign companies give territory in which incorporated.)*

Unless otherwise arranged with Land Registry headquarters, a certified copy of the transferee's constitution (in English or Welsh) will be required if it is a body corporate but is not a company registered in England and Wales or Scotland under the Companies Acts.

8. Transferee's intended address(es) for service in the U.K. *(including postcode)* **for entry on the register**

---

9. The Transferor transfers the Property to the Transferee.

10. Consideration *(Place 'X' in the box that applies. State clearly the currency unit if other than sterling. If none of the boxes applies, insert an appropriate memorandum in the additional provisions panel.)*

☐ The Transferor has received from the Transferee for the Property the sum of *(in words and figures)*

☐ *(insert other receipt as appropriate)*

☐ The transfer is not for money or anything which has a monetary value

11. The Transferor transfers with *(place "X" in the box which applies and add any modifications)*

☐ full title guarantee   ☐ limited title guarantee

12. Declaration of trust *Where there is more than one transferee, place X in the appropriate box.*

☐ The Transferees are to hold the Property on trust for themselves as joint tenants.

☐ The Transferees are to hold the Property on trust for themselves as tenants in common in equal shares.

☐ The transferees are to hold the Property *(complete as necessary)*

13. Additional Provisions

1. Use this panel for:
- *definitions of terms not defined above*
- *rights granted or reserved*
- *restrictive covenants*
- *other covenants*
- *agreements and declarations*
- *other agreed provisions*
- *required or permitted statements, certificates or applications.*

2. The prescribed subheadings may be added to, amended, repositioned or omitted.

Definitions

Rights granted for the benefit of the Property

Rights reserved for the benefit of other land *(the land having the benefit should be defined, if necessary by reference to a plan)*

Restrictive covenants by the Transferee *(include words of covenant)*

Restrictive covenants by the Transferor *(include words of covenant)*

14. *The Transferors and all other necessary parties (including the proprietors of all the titles listed in panel 3) should execute this transfer as a deed using the space below and sign the plan. Forms of execution are given in Schedule 3 to the Land Registration Rules 1925. If the transfer contains transferees' covenants or declarations or contains an application by them (e.g. for a restriction), it must also be executed by the Transferees.*

Form DS1

**Cancellation of entries
relating to a
registered charge**
*This form should be accompanied
by either Form API or Form DS2*

HM Land Registry

DS1

(If you need more room than is provided for in a panel use continuation sheet CS and staple to this form)

1. Title Number(s) of the Property

2. Property

3. Date

4. Date of charge

5. Lender

6. The Lender acknowledges that the property is no longer charged as security for the payment of sums due under the charge.

7. Date of Land Registry facility letter (if any)

8. *To be executed as a deed by the lender or in accordance with the above facility letter.*

Form END1

**Electronic Notification
For Discharge (END)**

END1

Lender's Name: Halifax plc Lender's Address: Trinity Road, Halifax, HX1 2RG	

Conveyancer Name Address	Our Ref. _____
	Telephone No. _____
	Fax No. _____
	E. mail _____

Funds sent to the lender by
☐ CHAPS ☐ CHEQUE ☐ EURO CHQ ☐ BACS

PROPERTY AND CHARGE DETAILS
*(if more than one charge is being redeemed use a separate form
for second and subsequent charges to the lender)*

Title Number	_____
Charge Date	_____
Borrower(s)	_____
Mortgage Account Number	_____
Additional Information	_____

ADDITIONAL SECURITY *(if any)*
Policy Assignments etc. YES/NO *(delete as applicable)*

FOR LENDERS USE ONLY

Date Funds Received	_____
Authority to release	_____
Input by	_____
Receipt of ENDs by HMLR checked	_____ Date _____

Confirmation *(the lender may use a separate form of receipt)*
**The Lender confirms that an END in respect of the charge detailed above has been lodged
with HM Land Registry.**
Signed on behalf of the lender _____
Date _____ Reference _____

Inland Revenue Stamps L(A)451

Inland Revenue

PARTICULARS OF INSTRUMENTS TRANSFERRING OR LEASING LAND

SECTION 28 FINANCE ACT 1931
as amended by the Land Commission Act 1967
and Section 89 Finance Act 1985

FOR OFFICIAL USE

VO No. ....

PD No. ....

ANALYSIS CODE ....

DESC ....

GV/NAV ....

DW CODE ....

RETURN ....

O.S. No. ....

OTHER ....

1. Description of Instrument
   Transfer

2. Date of Instrument
   12th July 1996

3. Name and address of Transferor or Lessor *(Block Letters)*
   RODNEY STEVEN CLAYTON and
   PATRICIA MARIA CLAYTON
   both of Hatherleigh Farmhouse
   Saxmundham Road
   Framlingham Woodbridge Suffolk

4. Name and address of Transferee or Lessee *(Block Letters)*
   BRIAN CLIFFORD GARRATT
   of The School
   Parham
   Woodbridge
   Suffolk

5. Situation of the land. Sufficient information must be given to enable the land to be identified accurately, e.g., by including any dimensions stated in the instrument and by attaching a plan to this form or by describing the boundaries in full. For premises the full postal address including the post code is required   Please indicate whether a plan is provided in the appropriate box.

   Hatherleigh Farmhouse Saxmundham Road Framlingham

   Plan Attached Yes ☑
   Plan Attached No ☐

   COUNTY Suffolk .... RATING AUTHORITY Suffolk Coastal District Council

6. Estate or Interest Transferred. Where the transaction is the assignment or grant of a lease, or the transfer of a fee simple subject to a lease, the terms of the lease, the date of commencement of the term and the rent reserved must be stated.

   freehold

7. Consideration   State separately: £250,000.00

   (a) any capital payment, with the date when due if otherwise than the execution of instrument:

   (b) does the consideration stated include a charge to VAT

   Yes/No   No

   If Yes please state the amount paid:

   (c) any debt released, covenanted to be paid or to which the transaction is made subject: NIL

   (d) any periodical payment (including any charge) covenanted to be paid: NIL

   (e) any terms surrendered: NIL

   (f) any land exchanged: NIL

   (g) any other thing representing money or money's worth: NIL

8. Any Minerals, Mineral Rights, Sporting Rights, Timber or Easements reserved: (on a separate sheet if necessary)   NIL

9. Any Restrictions, Covenants or Conditions affecting the value of the estate or interest transferred or granted: (on a separate sheet if necessary)   NIL

10. Signature of Transferee or Lessees or person on his behalf:

    Ross Coates   Date 12th July 1996

11. Name and Address of the Transferor's or Lessor's Solicitor: *(Block Letters)*
    Ross Coates
    Solicitor
    139 Main Road
    Kesgrave
    IPSWICH Suffolk IP5 7NP
    STAMPS L(A) 451 (3/95)

12. Name, Address and Telephone Number of Signatory *if other than Transferee or Lessee:* *(Block Letters)*
    Ling & Co.
    5 Bridge Street
    Framlingham
    Woodbridge
    Suffolk

Form FR1

First Registration
Application

HM Land Registry

FR1

(if you need more room than is provided for in a panel, use continuation sheet CS and staple to this form)

---

1. Administrative area

2. Superior title *(if any)* | **Deposit No.** *(if any)*

3. Address (including postcode) or other description of the property to be registered

On registering a rentcharge, show the address as follows:- 'Rentcharge over 2 The Grove, Anytown, Northshire NE2 900'

4. Extent to be registered *(place 'X' in the appropriate box)*

☐ The property is fully identified on the plan to the   *(enter nature and date of deed)*

☐ The property is fully identified on the attached plan and shown   *(enter reference e.g. 'edged red')*

☐ The description in panel 3 is sufficient to enable the property to be fully identified on the OS map.

Application, Priority and Fees Nature of applications in **priority order**	Value/premium £	Fees paid £	**FOR OFFICIAL USE ONLY** Record of fees paid
1. **First Registration of the property**			
2.			
3.			**Particulars of under/over payments**
4.			
		TOTAL £	

Accompanying cheques or postal orders should be made payable to 'HM Land Registry'.

6. The title applied for is *(place 'X' in the appropriate box)*

☐ absolute freehold   ☐ absolute leasehold   ☐ good leasehold   ☐ possessory freehold   ☐ possessory leasehold

7. Application lodged by

Land Registry Key No. 3753706

Name Ross Coates

Address/DX No. DX123922 Framlingham

Reference SB/

FOR OFFICIAL USE ONLY State Codes

Telephone No. (01728) 723509 | Fax. No. (01728) 723709

8. Where the Registry is to deal with someone else
*The Registry will send any land/charge certificate to the person named in panel 7 above and will, if necessary, contact that person.
You can change this by placing 'X' against one or more of the statements and completing the details on Form DL.*

☐ Please send any land/charge certificate to the person shown in panel 2 on Form DL

☐ Please raise any requisitions or queries with the person shown in panel 2 on Form DL

☐ Please send the document(s) listed in panel 3 on Form DL to the person shown in panel 2

9. Full name(s) and address(es) within the U.K. (including postcode) for service of notices and correspondence **of every owner of the land** *Where the owner is a company include Company's Registered Number if any: for Scottish Co. Reg. Nos., use an SC prefix. For foreign company give territory in which incorporated.*

Unless otherwise arranged with Land Registry headquarters, a certified copy of the owner's constitution (in English or Welsh) will be required if it is a body corporate but is not a company registered in England and Wales or Scotland under the Companies Acts.

10. *Where the owners are joint proprietors, place 'X' in the appropriate box.*

☐ The owners are holding the property on trust for themselves as joint tenants.

☐ The owners are holding the property on trust for themselves as tenants in common in equal shares.

☐ The owners are holding the property *(complete as necessary)*

11. The title is based on the title documents listed on Form DL which are all those which the applicant holds or has control of. Place 'X' in the *appropriate box. If applicable complete the second statement; include any interests disclosed only by searches. Any interests disclosed by searches which do not affect the land being registered should be certified.*

☐ All rights, interests and claims affecting the property known to the applicant are disclosed in the title documents. There is no-one in adverse possession of the property or any part of it.

☐ In addition to the rights, interests and claims affecting the property disclosed in the title documents, the applicant only knows of the following:

Information in respect of a chargee or mortgagee
Do not give this information if a Land Registry MD reference is printed on the charge, unless the charge has been transferred Full name and address within the U.K. (including postcode) for the service of notices and correspondence of the present proprietor of each charge or mortgage to be registered. Where the proprietor is a company include Company's Registered Number if any; for Scottish Co. Reg. Nos., use an SC prefix. For foreign companies give territory in which incorporated.

Unless otherwise arranged with Land Registry headquarters, the following documents are required:
(i) the original and a certified copy of any incorporated documents as defined in r. 139, Land Registration Rules 1925;
(ii) a certified copy of the chargee's constitution (in English or Welsh) if it is a body corporate but is not a company registered in England and Wales or Scotland under the Companies Acts.

13. *Place 'X' in this box if you are NOT able to give this certificate* ☐
I/We have investigated or caused to be investigated the title in the usual way on the applicant's behalf on a transaction for value.

14. I/We confirm that we have authority to lodge this application and request the Registrar to complete the registration.

Signature(s) of person
lodging this form _____ **Date** _____
(A form lodged by solicitors/licensed conveyancers must be signed in the firm's name)

N.B. Failure to complete the form honestly and with proper care may deprive the applicant of protection under the Land Registration Acts if as a result, a mistake is made in the register. Any dealing with the land not lodged with this form must be lodged with the appropriate application form and will take priority from the day it is deemed to be delivered.

This form is not part of the statutory form. Its completion is voluntary. No individual property or person will be identifiable from the information collected. The information will be used to improve the Registry's forecasting and its published Price Reports and may be supplied to the Office of National Statistics.

The property is
☐ a single residential property with vacant possession

It is a ☐ secondhand ☐ new ☐ newly converted

☐ flat/maisonette ☐ terraced house ☐ semi-detached house ☐ detached house

with ☐ no more than one ☐ two ☐ three ☐ four ☐ five or more bedrooms

☐ other residential

☐ non residential

Form AP1

Application to change the register

HM Land Registry

AP1

(if you need more room than is provided for in a panel, use continuation sheet CS and staple to this form)

---

1. Administrative area(s) and postcode *(if known)*

2. Title Number(s)

Deposit No. *(if any)*

3. Application, Priority and Fees

Nature of applications in priority order

Value £   Fees paid £

FOR OFFICIAL USE ONLY
Record of fees paid

1.
2.
3.
4.
5.
6.

Particulars of under/over payments

TOTAL £

A. ~mpanying cheques or postal orders should be made payable to "HM Land Registry".

4. Documents lodged with this form

1.	2.	3.
4.	5.	6.
7.	8.	9.
10.	11.	12.
13.	14.	15.

5. Application lodged by

Land Registry Key No. 3753706
Name Moving Direct
Address/DX No.
DX124721

Reference

FOR OFFICIAL USE ONLY
Codes
Dealing

Status

Telephone No. (01473) 464444   Fax No. (01473) 740444

6. Where the Registry is to deal with someone else

The Registry will send any land/charge certificate to the person named in panel 5 above and will, if necessary, contact that person. You can change this by placing "X" against one or more of the statements and completing the details below.

☐ Please send any land/charge certificate to the person shown below

☐ Please raise any requisitions or queries with the person shown below

☐ Please issue to the person shown below the following document(s)

If you have placed 'X' against any statement above, complete the following name and address details:

Name

Address/DX No.

Reference   Telephone No.

P.T.O.

Form AS1

Assent of whole
of registered title(s)

HM Land Registry AS1

(if you need more room than is provided for in a panel use a continuation sheet C.S and staple to this form)

1. Title Number(s) of the Property (leave *blank if not yet registered*

2. Property

If this assent is made under section 37 of the Land Registration Act 1925 following a not-yet-registered dealing with part only of the land in a title or is made under rule 72 of the Land Registration Rules 1925 include a reference to the last preceding document of title containing a description of the property.

3. Date

4. Name of deceased proprietor *(give full names)*

5. Personal Representative of deceased proprietor *(give full names and Company's Registered Number if any)*

6. Recipient **for entry on the register** *(Give full names and Company's registered Number if any: for Scottish Co. Reg. Nos. use an –S(:Prefix. I or foreign companies give territory in which incorporated.)*

Unless otherwise arranged with Land Registry headquarters a certified copy of the transferee's constitution (in English or Welsh) will be required if it is a body corporate but is not a t company registered in England and Wales or Scotland under the Companies Acts.

7. Recipient's intended address(es) for service in the U.K. *(including postcode)* for entry on the register

8. **The Personal Representative assents to the vesting of the property in the Recipient.**

9. The Personal Representative assents with *(place X in the bar which applies and add any modifications)*

|~ *full title guarantee* |~ limited title guarantee

10. Declaration of trust *Where there is more than one recipient place X in the appropriate box.*

|~ The recipients are to hold the property on trust for themselves as joint tenants.
|| The recipients are to hold the property on trust for themselves as tenants in common in equal shares.
[~ The recipients are to hold the property *(complete as necessary)*

Completion statement

COMPLETION STATEMENT

Purchase of Hatherleigh Farmhouse Saxmundham Road Framlingham Suffolk

Purchase price	53,000.00	Anticipated Mortgage Advance	50,350.00
Fees of Ross Coates to include VAT at 17.5%	182.07	Deposit paid	2,650.00
Local Authority and Water Authority search fees	77.63		
Land Registry and Land Charges searches	7.00	Balance required to complete	386.70
Telegraphic Transfer fee	20.00		
Land Registration fee	100.00		
	<u>53,386.70</u>		<u>53,386.70</u>

Instructions to act on sale/purchase of freehold/leasehold property

Property

1   Date received:

2   Client: seller/buyer/mortgagor/mortgagee

Name:

Address:

Occupation:

Phone   Office: Home:

3   Old client/introduced by:

4   Seller/buyer:

5   Seller's/buyer's conveyancers:

6   Estate agent:

7   Price:

8   Fittings etc included:

9   Preliminary deposit: £   paid to:

10   Deposit arrangements:

Seller

11   Title documents:

12   Local search, notices:

13   Deposit:

14   Linked sale and purchase:

15   Receipts:

16   Planning consents:

17   Plans:

18   Insurance:

19   On sale of a flat:
- get lease:
- outgoings:
- maintenance accounts:
- insurance:
- management co shares:
- lessor's licence:
- grant of a new lease:

20   Replies to National Protocol forms:

21   Possession:

22   Mortgage to repay?

Buyer

23   Deposit:

24   Instructions for search:

25   Linked sale and purchase:

26   Joint purchase:

27   Insurance:

28   Mortgage arrangements:

29   Survey arrangements:

30   Life insurance:

31   If available, go through special conditions of sale, lease, replies to National Protocol forms.

Both parties

32   Other terms:

33   Cost estimate:

34   Instructions for will?

Conveyancing agendas

Before completion

Seller/mortgagor

1   Deposit pd us/agents.

2   Get last rects/title deeds.

3   Arrange discharge of mtge.

4   Arrange exchange of contracts by telephone.

5   Send client prelims/requons to check.

6   Take up refs.

7   Get licence to assign.

8   Prepare: (a) sched of docs; (b) list re outgoings, to discharge mtge, to obtain NHBC cert; (c) authy to tenant(s); (d) LR Form 53/staty rect/withd N/dep; (e) Co Form 395; (f) Co. resns; (g) LR cover; (h) notice to lessor of mtge; (i) share transfer; (j) B/C.

9   Write out requirets.

10 Get exd by client: mtge/transfer/lease/Form 53/staty rect/withd N dep/authy to tenants/Co Form 395/rect for chattel money/unds to pay outgoings; share transfer/ctpt licence to assign/notice to lessor of mtge.

11 Keys arrange release to byr.

12 Confirm all mtgee's requirements satisfied.

13 Arrange completion by post or credit transfer (telephone or CHAPS).

Buyer/mortgagee

1   Deposit pd seller's solrs/agents.

2   Confirm replies satisfactory to searches etc.

3   Arrange exchange of contracts by telephone.

4   Take up refs.

5   Check replies to National Protocol forms.

6   Exchange contracts.

7   Examine deeds.

8   Requisitions on title.

9   Draft transfer/mtge.

10   Insurance.

11   Prepare: (a) rel of dep; (b) Form L(A); (c) und re outgoings, repairs (d) rect for chattel money; (e) Co Form 395; (f) Co resns; (g) LR cover; (h) R/T; (i) ctpt licence to assign; (j) notices to lessor of asst/mtge; (k) share transfer; (l) notice to insce soc; (m) B/C; (n) assignment of life policy.

12   Write with complon requirements.

13   Get complon money, costs, from client.

14   Get mtge advance.

15   Get exd by client: transfer/ctpt lease/mtge/unds.

16   Obtain banker's drafts or arrange TT.

17   Make final searches.

18   Confirm all BS/LA/bank/mtgee's requirements satisfied.

19   Arrange completion by credit transfer (telephone or CHAPS).

Completion

1   Inspect/produce deeds/land or charge certe/last rects.

2   Get/hand over transfer/lease/licence to assign/title docs/land or charge certe (requon no   ).

3   Get/hand over und to discharge mtge/LR Form 53/staty rect/withd N dep/consent to dealing.

4   Get/hand over rel of dep/ctpt lease/sched of docs/share certe and transfer/NHBC certe, agreement or und re do.

6   Get/hand over und as to outgoings, repairs/ctpt licence to assign.

7   Get/hand over authy to tenant(s)/keys/licence to assign/fire pol (endd)/rect for chattel money/Co Form 395/Co resns.

8   Endorse memo of sale on.

9   Get/give deposit no of land certe.

10   Get/hand over.

11   Complete drafts and mtge blanks.

12   Get banker's drafts or by TT for £   and £

13   Pay seller/mtgor/mtgee (redem).
        • draft or by TT £   .
        • draft or by TT £   .

14   Or transfer direct to seller's clients' account £   by phone
        or TT.

After completion

1   Write seller/buyer reporting complon; re dep; re insce (and
        recover all premiums); with B/C; with cheque/copy mtge/last
        rect, etc; re keys; re deeds; re will

2   Write mtgee/bank reporting complon; with cheque; with Form
        53 or staty rect; with fire pol etc.

3   L(A) and stamp convce/transfer/asst/lease/share transfer.

4   Register with Regr of Cos Co Form 395.

5   Register asst/mtge/with lessor's solr and pay fee.

6   Register share transfer.

7   Register in LR transfer/lease/withd of N of dep/Form 53/mtge/N
        deposit/notice of option in lease.

8   Write estate agent re deposit.

9   Lodge sllr's land certe in LR; give/get dep no.

10   Write insce soc of bldg soc's interest in life endowment policy.

11   Write insce soc re byr's/mtgee's interest in fire policy/surrender
        policy.

12   Notice to local authority and water authority.

13   Send NHBC form.

14   Credit seller's banking account with £   .

15   Get costs; pay or transfer to office bank account.

16   Send ctpt licence to assign to lessor's solr.

17   Diarise land registration due date.

15 Further Reading

The most authoritative work in this field is *Emmet on Title* (looseleaf, FT Law & Tax).

Other works which take the material contained in this book further are:

Aldridge, T, *Boundaries, Walls and Fences*, 7th edn, 1992, London: FT Law & Tax

Coates, RM, *Practical Conveyancing – Residential Commercial and Agricultural*, 13th edn, 1995, London: FT Law & Tax

Colbey, R, *Practice Notes on Residential Tenancies*, 4th edn, 2001, London: Cavendish Publishing

Harwood, M, *Conveyancing Law and Practice*, 2nd edn, 1996, London: Cavendish Publishing

Sawyer, C and Kerwal, L, *Contemporary Property Law*, forthcoming, 2002, London: Cavendish Publishing

Silverman, F, *Searches and Enquiries: A Conveyancer's Guide*, 2nd edn, 1992, London: Butterworths

Silverman, F, *Standard Conditions of Sale: A Conveyancer's Guide*, 6th edn, 1999, Tolley

Timothy, PJ, *Wontner's Guide to Land Registry Practice*, 19th edn, 1995, London: FT Law & Tax

Tolley's Value Added Tax 2000–2001, 2nd edn, 2000, Bath

Tolley's Stamp Duties and Stamp Duty Reserve Tax 1999–2000, 7th edn, Surrey

Wilkinson, GHW, *Pipes, Mains, Cables and Sewers*, 6th edn, 1995, London: FT Law & Tax

Wilkinson, HW, *Standard Conditions of Sale*, 5th edn, 1990, FT Law & Tax.

For addresses of district land registries and the land charges department areas served by district land registries and areas of compulsory registration, see *Costs and Fees Service* (looseleaf, FT Law & Tax).

For addresses of local authorities, see *Directory of Local Authorities*, 1999 edn, 1999, London: Sweet & Maxwell.